E̶v̶e̶r̶y̶ ̶d̶a̶y̶ ̶n̶o̶w̶

b̶r̶o̶u̶g̶h̶t̶ ̶m̶e̶ nearer

my freedom ̶a̶n̶d̶ ̶I̶

...nearer

my freedom...

The INTERESTING LIFE of

OLAUDAH EQUIANO by HIMSELF

MONICA EDINGER *and* LESLEY YOUNGE

ZEST BOOKS
MINNEAPOLIS

For Daisy —M.E.

For those I've taught and
those who've taught me —L.Y.

Zest Books™
An imprint of Lerner Publishing Group, Inc.
241 First Avenue North
Minneapolis, MN 55401 USA

For reading levels and more information, look up this title at www.lernerbooks.com.
Visit us at zestbooks.net. 🅵 📷

Designed by Athena Currier.
Main body text set in Bulmer MT Std.
Typeface provided by Monotype Typography.

Library of Congress Cataloging-in-Publication Data

Names: Edinger, Monica, 1952– author. | Younge, Lesley, author.
Title: Nearer my freedom : the interesting life of Olaudah Equiano by himself / Monica Edinger and Lesley Younge.
Description: Minneapolis : Zest Books , [2023] | Includes bibliographical references and index. | Audience: Ages 10–18 | Audience: Grades 7–9 | Summary: "Using Olaudah Equiano's autobiography as the source, the text shares Equiano's life story in found verse. Readers will follow his story from his childhood in Africa, enslavement at a young age, liberation, and life as a free man" —Provided by publisher.
Identifiers: LCCN 2022023681 (print) | LCCN 2022023682 (ebook) | ISBN 9781728450988 (library binding) | ISBN 9781728464077 (paperback) | ISBN 9781728462721 (ebook)
Subjects: LCSH: Equiano, Olaudah, 1745–1797. | Slaves—Biography—Juvenile literature.
Classification: LCC HT869.E6 E35 2023 (print) | LCC HT869.E6 (ebook) | DDC 306.3/62092 [B]—dc23/eng/20220718

LC record available at https://lccn.loc.gov/2022023681
LC ebook record available at https://lccn.loc.gov/2022023682

Manufactured in the United States of America
1-50633-50069-10/7/2022

Table of Contents

About This Book

ACCORDING TO HIS AUTOBIOGRAPHY, OLAUDAH EQUIANO WAS born in West Africa in 1745, kidnapped from his village at a young age, shipped across the ocean, and sold into slavery as part of the Atlantic triangular trade system. This traumatic set of events launched him on a series of incredible adventures that would be extraordinary for anyone—especially for someone who was enslaved. Equiano spent very little of his time on land working in agriculture like the majority of captured Africans. Instead, he was primarily at sea on British military and merchant ships. His experiences as a sailor afforded him unique opportunities, of which he took every advantage.

Despite his circumstances, Olaudah Equiano never lost sight of his desire for freedom, and he was eventually able to pay for his own liberation. Afterward, he moved to England and integrated himself into British society. Known for most of his life as Gustavus Vassa, Olaudah was a sailor, a gentleman, an adventurer, a merchant, and a hairdresser before becoming a writer and the first best-selling author of African descent in the Western world. He sailed across the Atlantic Ocean many times and traveled along other waterways, including the Arctic Ocean and the Mediterranean Sea. Known for his integrity and intelligence, he was asked to help with various projects, such as building a plantation in Honduras and setting up a colony of free Black people in Sierra Leone. He established a reputation as a writer and orator. Ultimately, Equiano became a significant figure in the multiracial abolition movement that swept across England in the late eighteenth and early nineteenth centuries.

Slavery is—and has always been—a global industry that creates wealth for generations of traders, consumers, and enslavers around the world. Many would like to forget or erase this uncomfortable fact, yet the truth persists. This book focuses specifically on slavery and abolition through the eyes and words of Olaudah Equiano, whose aim was freedom. Equiano spent much of his life enslaved under the British Empire's laws, yet he freed himself. His words and advocacy also freed others from accepting slavery as if it were an inevitable part of economic systems. By speaking the truth, he created a path for himself and many others to choose and forge a brighter future.

In many ways, the transatlantic slave trade was a particularly cruel form of slavery. Repercussions from it still ripple through our societies today. Olaudah Equiano's story makes clear that slavery was a complex and profitable international business. It is difficult to separate the modern-day wealth and power of countries like the United States, Britain, France, the Netherlands, Sweden, Denmark, Spain, and Portugal from their early reliance on the slave trade and the labor of enslaved people.

Here we present a verse version of Olaudah Equiano's powerful first-person account. Found verse takes existing text and reorganizes a selection of words, phrases, and sentences into poems. The poems use *The Interesting Narrative of the Life of Olaudah Equiano, or Gustavus Vassa, the African, Written by Himself* as the source text. This book helped birth a genre of literature and was a powerful tool against the institution of slavery. By listening to and honoring this voice from the past, we can draw inspiration from a historical figure who tenaciously pursued the liberation of himself and others. By bearing witness to a trauma experienced by over ten million people, you are more prepared to join the modern-day pursuit for justice, reconciliation, and abolition.

A Note on Language

OLAUDAH EQUIANO WAS AN EXCELLENT WRITER, AND USING HIS autobiography as a source text helps preserve the eloquence of his voice while remixing it into poetry that uses various forms and devices. You may notice that some words are unfamiliar because they are no longer used by modern English speakers. Others appear with their British spellings, such as "colour." In the informational sections, we used modern terms such as "Black," "enslaved person," and "enslaver" rather than the terms Equiano uses in his book such as "Negro," "slave," or "master," which were the accepted vocabulary of the time.

To the Parliament of Great Britain:

My Lords and Gentlemen,

Permit me to lay at your feet
the following genuine
Narrative,

to excite a sense of compassion
for my unfortunate countrymen.

When the question of Abolition is to be discussed,
thousands are to look for Happiness or Misery,
in consequence of your Determination.

Your most
obedient
devoted
humble
servant,

Olaudah Equiano, or Gustavus Vassa
March 24, 1789

Part One

CHAPTER ONE
I Was Born in Essaka

1.
I was born
in that part of Guinea, Africa,
that extends along the coast
from Senegal to Angola,
where the trade for slaves is carried on.

I was born
in the kingdom of Benin,
the most considerable as to
wealth,
      richness,
           warlike inhabitants,
and the power of its king.

I was born
in the year 1745
in a charming fruitful vale called Essaka,
in a province called Eboe,
remote and fertile.

I was born
and named Olaudah, signifying
fortune and one favoured,
having a loud voice,
and well spoken.

I was born
never hearing of:
white men,
Europeans,
nor of the sea.

2.
We are a nation of
dancers, musicians, poets.

Every great event
every triumphant return from battle
celebrated with songs and public dances.

Our manners are simple,
our luxuries few,
our wants easily supplied.

Our land: uncommonly rich and fruitful,
all kinds of vegetables in great abundance.
Agriculture is our chief employment.
Others spin and weave cotton,
manufacture earthen vessels and tobacco pipes.

We have no beggars. Everyone,
even children and women,
labour from our earliest years.

Our dress: both sexes the same
calico or muslin, a long piece
wrapped loosely around the body,
usually dyed blue,
our favorite color extracted from a berry,
brighter and richer than any I've seen in Europe
Our women wear golden
ornaments on their arms and legs.

Our food: bullocks, goats, and poultry
stewed in a pan with pepper, other spices,
a salt made of wood ashes.
Plantains, eadas, yams, beans, and Indian corn.
Before we taste,
we always wash our hands.
Our cleanliness, an indispensable ceremony.
After washing, libation.
A small portion of drink on the floor
for the spirits of departed relations
guarding us from evil.

Our buildings: one-story wood houses
plastered within and without
walls and floors covered with mats,
roof thatched with reeds.
Each master of a family
has a large square piece of land,

surrounded with moat or fence,
sufficient to accommodate his family and slaves
who do no more
than others of the community,
their food, clothing, and lodging—nearly the same.

Our religion: one Creator
who governs all things and lives in the sun.
He may never eat or drink
but smokes a pipe.
We've no places of public worship
but priests, magicians, and wisemen
calculate time, foretell events,
and are held in great reverence.

Such is the imperfect memory sketch
of the manners and customs
of a people among whom I first drew breath.

Olaudah Equiano's West Africa

OLAUDAH EQUIANO SAYS HE WAS BORN IN WEST AFRICA IN AN Igbo province of the kingdom of Benin. The powerful kingdom of Benin was in the southern part of what is now Nigeria. It was an advanced civilization. Benin's artisans were highly skilled at their craft. They made beautiful objects from gold, bronze, ivory, and iron, many of which can still be seen in museums today. A Portuguese ship captain wrote this description in 1691:

> Great Benin, where the king resides, is larger than Lisbon; all the streets run straight and as far as the eye can see. The houses are large, especially that of the king, which is richly decorated and has fine columns. The city is wealthy and industrious. It is so well governed that theft is unknown and the people live in such security that they have no doors to their houses.

West Africa at that time was made up of many different kingdoms and groups of people whose alliances and conflicts ebbed and flowed. People who lived along the coast had been in contact with Europeans for centuries by the time Olaudah Equiano was captured. Goods produced by African artisans were traded along with captive people who were being taken to the Americas.

There is some debate about whether Equiano was actually born in Africa because there are some historical documents where he listed South Carolina as his birthplace. He may not have told people of his African birthplace or birth name until later in life. It is noted that the details of his autobiography and experiences largely match with other verifiable accounts and records,

Equiano's birthplace, the Benin Kingdom, is shown on this 1625 map of Guinea and the surrounding area, labeled as "Benin Regnu" (*far right*).

and it seems unlikely that he would give a false account of his birth yet be truthful about the rest.

These discrepancies aside, his description of West Africa provides us with accurate details about the area that are important to understand today. People who supported the slave trade often argued that Africans were better off enslaved because they had access to Christian teachings and to the "civilized" ways of Europeans. Equiano's description tells us about the loving families, safe homes, and rich cultures from which enslaved people were torn. For those working in abolitionist circles, his account offered very convincing evidence that the slave trade was wrong.

3.

My father was one of the elders or chiefs,
a mark of grandeur on his forehead.
Destined was I to receive it.

He had a family of seven, including myself
and a sister, the only daughter,
and many slaves.

I was the youngest son,
the favourite of my mother,
and always with her.

My daily exercise was shooting
and throwing javelins. I was trained
from my earliest years in the art of war.

All are taught the use of weapons: firearms,
bows and arrows, broad two-edge swords
shields that cover a man from head to foot.

Even our women march boldly!
Our whole district—a militia.
All rise and rush upon their enemy.

My mother adorned me
with emblems of our greatest warriors.
She took particular pains to form my mind.

In this way I grew up
till the age of eleven, when an end
was put to my happiness.

4.

Our markets were visited
by mahogany-coloured men from the southwest.
Oye-Eboe: red men living at a distance.

They brought such European goods as
       hats,
       dried fish,
       fire-arms,
       gunpowder,
       and beads.

Through our land they carried slaves.
We asked how they procured them
before they were suffered to pass.

Sometimes we sold slaves to them, but
only prisoners of war or those convicted
of kidnapping and other heinous crimes.

Notwithstanding our strictness,
I think their principal business
was to kidnap our people.

They carried great sacks, which not long after
I had an opportunity of seeing applied
to that infamous purpose.

CHAPTER TWO
No Small Fear

5.
One day when none of the grown people were nigh
two men and a woman got over our walls,
seized my dear sister and me.
No time to cry out, or make resistance.

They stopped our mouths,
and ran off with us into the woods.
They tied our hands and carried us
as far as they could, till night came.

Overpowered by fatigue and grief,
our only relief: sleep
our only comfort: one another's arms
bathing each other with our tears.

We continued travelling and came to a road
I believed I knew with people at a distance.
My cries for assistance had them
stop my mouth, tie me faster, put me into a large sack.

The next day brought greater sorrow
than I had yet experienced.
My sister and I were separated.
In vain we sought them not to part us.

She was torn from me and carried away.
I was left in a state not to be described.

6.
I cried
and grieved continually.

Several days I did not eat
but what they forced
into my mouth.

After many days' travel,
I changed
into the hands of a chieftain
with two wives and some children.

Although many days from my father's house,
these people spoke the same language.
They did all they could to comfort me,
particularly the first wife
who was something like my mother.

This first master of mine, a smith,
my employment was working his bellows.
I believe it gold he worked—

a bright yellow colour—
worn by the women on their wrists and ankles.

They at last trusted me some
little distance from the house.
I remarked on where the sun rose
in the morning and set in the evening.
I observed that my father's house
was towards
the rising of the sun.

Oppressed and weighed down by grief,
my love of liberty great,
I determined to seize the first opportunity
of making my escape.

Slavery in Africa

SLAVERY IS AN ANCIENT PRACTICE THAT HAS EXISTED IN MANY societies and civilizations throughout time. As early as 1000 BCE, people in different parts of southern Africa were captured and sold to traders who took them to North Africa, Europe, and Asia. In Europe, members of lower socioeconomic classes were coerced into labor as feudal serfs, indentured servants, and apprentices. By the sixteenth century, Portugal had established the transatlantic slave trade, capturing Africans on behalf of Europeans.

Slavery existed within the cultures of eighteenth-century Africa as well. Warring groups might enslave and sell enemies they had captured. Someone might be enslaved as payment for a debt or punishment for a crime. Traders might also approach village leaders and entice them to attack and kidnap people from another village. Those who were enslaved in Africa might be considered property, or they might become part of the enslaver's family. They might be able to gain a position of power or to even enslave others. As with indentured servitude, it was possible to shed the status of slave and for one's children to be born free. This was different from the chattel slavery established in the Americas, under which the idea of race and racial hierarchy developed and became a justification for enslaving Africans specifically. Chattel slavery also made enslaved status permanent and hereditary, so that the children of someone who was enslaved were automatically enslaved for life too.

Olaudah Equiano's description of slavery in Africa shows the network of different people who were involved in the slave trade, which included Europeans, Arab traders from the North, and West Africans. European traders usually waited in coastal towns, on boats, and in slavery fortresses for captives to be brought to them from the interior lands. A network of local and foreign traders would bring captives to the coast. Some African leaders benefited from the slave trade and received valuable weapons, tools, and goods in exchange. Other leaders resisted and rebelled while trying to protect their people. As European colonization of North and South America increased, so did the demand for enslaved labor. Thus the transatlantic slave trade persisted for centuries, changing the cultural and political landscapes of Africa in many ways.

7.

One morning an unlucky event happened
putting an end to my hopes.
While feeding some chickens,
I tossed a pebble, which hit one
and killed it.

An old slave inquired after the chicken.
Since my mother would never suffer me to lie,
I told the truth.
She flew into a violent passion
and told her mistress.

Expecting a flogging, I ran and hid in the bushes.
My mistress searched the house.
Not finding me, the whole neighbourhood
was raised in the pursuit.
I expected every moment to be found out.

Most supposed I had fled towards home.
The distance was so great
the way so intricate,
they thought I could never reach it,
they thought I should be lost in the woods.
I heard this and was seized
with panic
      with despair
            with fear.

I had entertained hopes of home
but was now convinced it was fruitless.

If I could escape other animals,
I could not escape the human kind.
Thus, was I like the hunted deer.

Faint and hungry,
I crept to my master's kitchen,
and laid myself down in the ashes
with a wish for death.

In the morning when the old woman
came to light the fire,
she could scarcely believe her eyes.
She went for her master, who reprimanded me
and ordered me not to be ill-treated.

8.

Soon I was sold again
carried to the left of the sun's rising
through different countries
through dreary wastes
through dismal woods
amidst the roarings of wild beasts.

When I was tired, the people I was sold to
carried me on their shoulders or backs.

While journeying through Africa,
I acquired two or three different tongues.
The languages of different nations did not totally differ,
so were easily learned.

From the time I left my own nation
I always found *somebody* that understood me.

Until I came to the sea coast.

9.
One evening, a great surprise:
my dear sister brought
to the house where I was!

She ran into my arms.
We clung to each other
unable to do anything
but weep.

Our meeting affected
all who saw.
When these people knew
we were brother and sister,
they indulged us to be together.

All night
she and I held one another by the hands.
For a while we forgot our misfortunes
in the joy of being together.
But this was soon to have an end.

Scarcely had the morning appeared,
when she was again torn from me
forever.

I was now more miserable than before.
Her image riveted in my heart.
Neither time nor fortune
have been able to remove it.

10.
Again sold.
Again carried through a number of places.

After a considerable time, I came to Tinmah
in the most beautiful country I had yet seen,
extremely rich and many rivulets flowed through.
Here I first tasted sugar cane and cocoanuts,
which I thought superior to any nuts I tasted before.

The houses had commodious shades,
insides neatly plastered and white washed.
Their money: little white shells the size of a finger nail.
A wealthy widow bought me with
one hundred and seventy-two of them.
Her house, the finest I ever saw in Africa,
had a number of slaves to attend to her.

Washed and perfumed, led into her presence
I ate and drank before her and her son,
a young man my own age and size.
It filled me with astonishment that he
should suffer me, who was bound,
to eat with him, who was free.

Their language and customs resembled ours so nearly
we understood each other perfectly.

There were slaves daily to attend
my young master and I,
while we sported with other boys,
throwing darts and bows and arrows
as I had at home.

I passed two months in this resemblance
to my former happy state.
I began to think I was to be adopted.
I forgot my misfortunes.

Then all at once, delusion vanished.
My taste of joy reversed.
One early morning I was awakened
and hurried away to fresh sorrow.

The Global Slave Trade

THE TRANSATLANTIC SLAVE TRADE, ALSO KNOWN AS THE ATLANTIC
slave trade, was a global industry that began in the 1400s. It was
part of a triangular trade system that involved routes to Africa,
Europe, and the Americas. When Europeans (including the Portuguese, Spanish, French, Dutch, and English) first invaded and
colonized the Western Hemisphere, they enslaved the Indigenous
people they came into contact with. But this proved difficult to
do on a large scale in the long term, as many Indigenous Americans fought back, ran away, or died from diseases spread by the

THE TRANSATLANTIC SLAVE TRADE

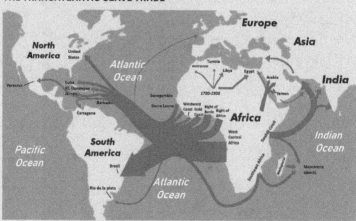

The majority of enslaved Africans were sent to the
Caribbean and South America. Smaller numbers of
people were captured and forced to North America,
North Africa, western Europe, and Asia.

colonizers. In some areas, fearing that the practice could lead to war with local groups, European colonizers passed laws against enslaving Indigenous people. Eventually, it became common practice to bring enslaved people from Africa against their will to do the work of building, farming, and collecting resources in the Americas. Over twelve million Africans were captured for this purpose between 1492 and 1870.

A very lucrative global economy was built upon the capture and enslavement of African people. Sugar, molasses, rum, tobacco, indigo, cotton, valuable wood like mahogany, and other agricultural products were grown, collected, and processed in the Americas and then taken to Europe. In Europe, these products were sold for manufactured goods, such as china, guns, and metalware. Manufactured goods traveled from Europe to Africa, where they were used to purchase people who could be sold and enslaved in the Americas to produce more crops and important raw materials. Around the world, people became rich from building the ships that carried enslaved people, owning the plantations where enslaved people worked, and running factories that processed the goods enslaved people produced.

11.

All the nations and people I had passed through,
in manners, customs, and language
resembled our own.

But I came at length to a country,
the inhabitants of which differed.
They cooked in iron pots
had European cutlasses
and crossbows.
These were unknown to us.

I came to the banks of a large river,
covered with canoes
in which the people appeared to live
with their household utensils
and provisions of all kinds.

Astonished!
I had never before seen water larger
than a pond or rivulet.

Some women and men would
     jump into the water,
               dive to the bottom,
                    come up again,
                         and swim.

My surprise mingled with no small fear
when I was put into one of these canoes.

We began to paddle and move along the river.

Marching to the Coast

ONCE PEOPLE WERE CAPTURED FROM THEIR VILLAGES IN WESTERN
Africa, their captors brought them to the coast. It could be an arduous journey, and death from thirst, hunger, and exhaustion was common. They might be brought directly to a ship or held at a slave fortress (also known as a slave factory), such as Elmina Castle in Ghana or Bunce Island in Sierra Leone. Bunce Island was the largest British slave fortress. It had crowded, filthy cells for the African captives, along with a two-hole golf course to entertain the European and American traders looking to buy and sell captives. Ships did not head out to sea until they were full, so once a captive was purchased by a trader, they might be kept on board in deadly conditions for weeks or months before the journey started. The ship would travel up and down the coast collecting more human cargo before beginning the ultimate journey: the Middle Passage across the Atlantic.

12.

I continued to travel,
by land,
by water,
through different countries and various nations,
till I arrived at the sea coast.

The first object that saluted my eyes was
the sea

a slave ship at anchor

waiting for its cargo.

13.

Astonishment converted to terror.
I was carried on board.
The crew tossed me up.
to see if I were sound.

Their complexions, long hair, and language
persuaded me
I was in a world of bad spirits
and they were going to kill me.

If ten thousand worlds had been my own,
I would have parted with them all
to exchange my condition with
the meanest slave in my own country.

I looked round the ship and saw
black people of every description
chained together, every one of their countenances
expressing dejection and sorrow.

I no longer doubted my fate.
Overpowered with horror and anguish,
I fainted and fell
motionless on the deck.

14.
When I recovered a little,
I found some black people about me.
I believed they were some of those
who brought me on board
and had been receiving their pay.

They talked to cheer me, but in vain.
I asked them if we were not to be eaten
by those white men with
horrible looks,
          red faces,
                and long hair.

They told me I was not,
went off, and left me
abandoned to despair.

I now saw myself deprived
of all chance
of gaining the shore

of returning to my native country
of the least glimpse of hope.

I wished for my former slavery,
in preference to my present situation
filled with horrors of every kind
and ignorance
of what I was to undergo.

15.
Under the decks, the loathsome
stench and crying
made me so sick and low
that I wished for death.

I had no desire to taste anything,
I refused to eat.
One white man
      held me fast by the hands
      laid me across the windlass
      flogged me severely.

Although I naturally feared the water,
could I have got over the nettings,
I would have jumped
           over the side
               into the sea.

Often did I think many inhabitants of the deep
much more happy than myself.
I envied their freedom.

16.

I found amongst the chained men
some of my own nation.
They eased my mind
and helped me understand
we were to be carried
to these white people's country to work.

Still, I feared I should be put to death.
The white people looked and acted
in a manner so savage,
I had never seen such cruelty.
This was not only shown towards blacks,
but also to some of the whites themselves.

I could not help my apprehensions:
Do these people have no country?
Do they live in this hollow ship?
How come we never heard of them?
Where are their women?
How does the vessel go?

They come from a different country.
They live so very far off.
Their women are left behind.
Cloths are put upon the masts and
some spell or magic is put in the water
in order to stop.

17.

Every circumstance served to heighten
my apprehensions of the cruelty of whites.

One day they had taken a number of fishes.
When they satisfied themselves
rather than give any to us to eat,
they tossed the remaining fish
into the sea.

We begged and prayed in vain.
Some of my countrymen, pressed by hunger,
tried to get a little when they thought no one saw.
They were discovered,
and flogged.

18.

Filth
Stench
Pestilential
Shrieks
Groans
Sickness
Death
Wretchedness
Suffocation
Miseries
Cruelty
Brutality
Fear

A Scene of Horror.

The Middle Passage

THE JOURNEY ACROSS THE ATLANTIC OCEAN, FROM AFRICA TO THE
Americas, which took anywhere from twenty-one to ninety days,
came to be called the Middle Passage. More than twelve million
Africans were taken aboard boats bound for markets across the
sea. British ships were responsible for carrying one-third of a
million people shipped during the 1780s. The trip took months. An
estimated 15 percent of people did not survive the journey. Since
they were considered goods and cargo instead of human beings,
the captives were kept in horrendous conditions, chained close
together within a small, confined space. Disease and death were
rampant. The enslaved Africans were often abused and violated
in terrible ways. Separated from their loved ones and unsure of
their immediate safety or chance at a future, many chose to jump
overboard to their deaths rather than continue being physically
and mentally tortured.

Olaudah Equiano describes his experience of the Middle Passage in terrifying detail:

> Now the whole ship's cargo were confined together, it became
> absolutely pestilential. The closeness of the place, and the heat
> of the climate, added to the number in the ship, which was so
> crowded that each had scarcely room to turn himself, almost suf-
> focated us. This produced copious perspirations, so that the air
> soon became unfit for respiration, from a variety of loathsome
> smells, and brought on a sickness among the slaves, of which
> many died. . . . The shrieks of the women, and the groans of the
> dying, rendered the whole scene a horror almost inconceivable.

The squalid conditions the captured Africans endured as they crossed the Atlantic made a compelling case for English abolitionists. They released a famous diagram of a crowded slave ship call the *Brookes* that shocked the public and politicians. They used vivid descriptions from former captives, sailors, and ships' doctors to convince British people that the slave trade was barbaric. A notorious court case regarding the murder of 132 captives on a ship called the *Zong* also raised outrage. Additionally, people were appalled to learn that 20 percent of British sailors died on these voyages. In response to public outcry, the British Parliament passed the 1788 Slave Trade Act, which limited the number of enslaved people who could be carried on a ship and required more humane treatment of captives. It was the first law that tried to regulate the trade, so it was seen by some as a sign of progress despite its imperfections.

19.

During our passage I first saw
flying fishes,
which surprised me.
Many fell on deck.

I also first saw the mariners
use the quadrant
and make observations with it.

They took note of my curiosity.
One made me look through it.
The clouds appeared
to be land, which disappeared
as they passed along.
This heightened my wonder.
I was now persuaded I was in another world,
everything about me magic.

20.

At last we came in sight of Barbados
at which the whites on board gave a great shout of joy.
In the harbour of Bridgetown ships of different kinds and sizes.
Anchored amongst them, merchants and planters came on board.

They made us jump and examined us attentively.
We thought we should be eaten by these ugly men.
There was much dread and trembling among us,
bitter cries all night.

Some old slaves from the land told us
we were not to be eaten but to work.
We were soon to go on land and
see many of our country people.

Sure enough, soon after we were landed
there came to us Africans of all languages.
In the merchant's yard, we were all penned up
together like so many sheep in a fold.

Colonization and the Caribbean Plantation System

OLAUDAH EQUIANO SPENT MANY YEARS TRAVELING AROUND THE Caribbean as both an enslaved person and a free sailor and merchant. Barbados and other Caribbean colonies were a critical part of the triangular transatlantic slave trade; 60 percent of all captured Africans were taken to this region.

Colonization of the area began with Christopher Columbus's fifteenth-century invasion, and European countries quickly began to fight for territory. Sometimes they were able to negotiate peacefully; other times they went to war. In the 1600s, Europeans colonizing islands in the Caribbean discovered that sugarcane grew well in the rich soil and tropical climate. It soon became an important and profitable crop.

The largest and most important British colonies were Jamaica and Barbados. In fact, in 1773 England imported five times more goods from Jamaica than it imported from all thirteen American colonies. These islands were ideal environments to grow sugar, which was in high demand as a sweetener for tea and coffee and even as a medicine. Molasses, a sugar product, was the primary ingredient in rum, a popular alcoholic beverage. Colonizers also grew tobacco, produced coffee, and cultivated livestock on the islands.

Sugar demanded a large workforce, and plantation owners found they made more money if they bought enslaved people instead of paying workers or indentured servants. Growing and processing large amounts of sugarcane was relentless and dangerous work. The death rate among enslaved workers in the Caribbean was higher than the birth rate. A constant stream of newly enslaved people replaced those who died.

Plantations were expensive to operate, so only the wealthiest merchants and landowners could afford to own them. Many of these plantation owners did not actually live on the islands at all. Instead, they stayed in Europe and collected the profits while managers and overseers supervised the daily operations, often with little care and great cruelty.

21.

We were not many
days in custody before
we were sold. At the
beat of a signal, a drum
some buyers rushed in the yard.

Their eagerness, noise
and clamour terrified us.
They made choice of that
they liked best without scruple.
Relations sadly parted.

Parents to lose their
children, brothers their sisters,
husbands their dear wives,
new cruelty, fresh horrors.
O, to see and hear their cries!

Arriving in Barbados

ONCE THE CAPTIVE AFRICANS ARRIVED IN THE AMERICAS AFTER THEIR terrible journey, they would be inspected and prepared for the slave markets. They would be cleansed, allowed to rest, and given more food in order to look healthier and more fit to work. Barbados had been one of the earliest British colonies and the first place where colonizers set up sugar cultivation. It had become a key outpost of the Atlantic slave trade because of its location in the eastern Caribbean, closer to Europe than other colonized islands.

Olaudah Equiano describes the chaos of these markets: the invasive inspections, merchants and buyers yelling at auctions, and the traumatic experience of not knowing what fate lay ahead. If they had managed to stay together so far, families could still be separated. Children and babies were often taken from their parents, never to be seen again. Once sold, a captive was legally the property of their enslaver. They could be taken anywhere and forced to do whatever work the enslavers wanted.

CHAPTER THREE
I Was Now amongst a People

22.
I now lost the small remains of comfort:
conversing with my countrymen
the women who cared for me

All were gone.
I never saw one of them afterwards.

After a few days, I and a few more slaves
not saleable on that island, were shipped
off in a sloop to North America.

On the passage we were better treated
than when we were coming from Africa.
We had plenty of rice and fat pork.

We were landed up a river, a good way
from the sea about Virginia county.

We saw few or none of our native Africans
and not one soul who could talk to me.

23.
Now on a Virginia plantation
Now called Jacob

I was born and named Olaudah

Now weeding grass and gathering stones
Now with no person I could understand

Now exceedingly miserable
Now constantly grieving

Now I wished for death.

The First Africans in Virginia

AFRICANS BEGAN LIVING IN VIRGINIA AS EARLY AS 1619, WHEN two English ships, the *White Lion* and the *Treasurer*, brought captive Africans to Point Comfort. At the time, England claimed this region as a colony. In the early years of American slavery, Africans labored alongside white indentured servants, building plantations of tobacco and eventually cotton. By 1662, slavery was becoming an institution. That year, the Virginia House of Burgesses passed a law declaring that the social status of a child depended on the status of their mother. If a child's mother was enslaved, the child would be too. Now slavery was hereditary and could continue for generations. Other colonies would also adopt this law. Not everyone in Virginia was an enslaver, but Virginia's economic system now favored people who owned a lot of land and a lot of people to work that land. Only these people were considered elite members of society. Aristocrats and future "Founding Fathers," such as George Washington and Thomas Jefferson, inherited and purchased enslaved adults and children who worked on their land and in their homes. This allowed them to gain further wealth and power.

Before slave auctions became the norm, enslavers would haggle with prospective buyers in exchange for food and goods, as depicted in this painting of an auction in Jamestown in 1619.

24.

One day, the gentleman to whom
the estate belonged was unwell.
I was sent to fan him.

Looking about, I was very much affrighted.
First, a watch hung on the chimney.
Surprised at the noise it made,
I was afraid it would tell the gentleman
anything I might do amiss.

Next, a picture hanging in the room
appeared to look at me constantly.
I thought it was magic, a way the whites had
to keep their great men when they died.

Then, a poor creature cooking dinner.
She was cruelly loaded with iron machines,
one on her head, which locked her mouth
so that she could scarcely speak, eat, or drink.

After some time, in this forlorn and much dejected state,
the kind hand of the Creator began to appear.

25.

One day the captain of a merchant ship,
a lieutenant in the royal navy,
came to my master's house:
      Michael Henry Pascal.

He liked me so well that he made a purchase of me
for thirty or forty pounds sterling
a present to some friends in England.

I was carried on board a large ship
loaded with tobacco and ready to sail for England.
I thought my condition much mended.
   Sails to lie on
   Plenty to eat
The white people used me kindly.
I began to think they were not all the same.

I could smatter a little imperfect English
and wanted to know where we were going.
They told me they were to carry me back.
   Back to my own country.

I rejoiced and thought if I should get home
what wonders I should have to tell.
But I was reserved for another fate
and undecieved when we came within sight
   of the English Coast.

26.
My master named me
Gustavus Vassa.

I would be Jacob
I told him.

You will not
he told me.

I refused to answer to my new name
gaining many a cuff.

At length I submitted,
Gustavus Vassa.
(I was born and named Olaudah)
by which name I have been known
ever since.

27.
On board was a lad who had
never been at sea before.
Richard Baker
a youth of a most amiable temper

who was four or five years older than myself
who was a native of America
who had many slaves of his own
who had received an excellent education
who showed me a great deal of attention.

At length we became inseparable,
and for two years he was my constant
companion, instructor, interpreter,
and faithful friend.

He had a mind superior to prejudice
not ashamed to associate
with a stranger of different complexion
with a stranger who was a slave.

28.

After thirteen weeks,
the ship arrived at Falmouth.
Every heart on board seemed gladdened,
none more than mine.

The captain went on shore
and sent on board some fresh provisions.
Our famine soon turned to feasting.

It was the spring of 1757 when I arrived in England.
I was near twelve years of age.

I was struck with the buildings and pavement.
Any object I saw filled me with new surprise.
One morning I got up on deck
and saw it covered with snow.

I thought it was salt.
I took up a handful, found it very cold,
tasted it, and was surprised beyond measure.

The mate asked if we had no such thing in my country.
No I told him no,
Who made it?

A great man in the heavens called God he told me.

I was at a loss to understand him.
A little after I saw the air filled with it,
a heavy shower.

Olaudah Equiano,
or Gustavus Vassa, the Writer

WHILE ENSLAVED PEOPLE OFTEN DESIRED TO LEARN TO READ AND write, few had access to this knowledge. In many places, teaching an enslaved person to read was against the law since such communication skills could be used to plan rebellions or escape. Olaudah Equiano was noteworthy because not only was he literate, but he also became a well-respected master of language and rhetoric. He published many public letters, editorials, and book reviews prior to writing his autobiography. He usually signed his work and referred to himself by his legal name, Gustavus Vassa, which was given to him by one of his enslavers, Captain Pascal, in homage to a sixteenth-century Swedish king. This legal name appeared on his manumission papers, but Equiano started to also refer to himself as "the African" and using Olaudah Equiano once he started his abolition work. Equiano's autobiography is considered exceptional because it was written by himself and made him "the first successful professional writer of African descent in the English-speaking world." His story was widely read when it was first published, and it still is today.

29.
I had often seen my master and Richard,
(whom I called Dick)
employed in reading.

I had a great curiosity to talk to the books,
as I thought they did.

When alone, I often took up a book,
talked to it
put my ears to it
hoped it would answer me.

I was very much concerned
when it remained silent.

30.
Once while he went to England,
my master placed me together with my friend Dick
to board and lodge with one of his mates,
who had a wife and family there.

This woman behaved to me
with great kindness and attention
and taught me everything in the same manner
as she did her own child.

This mate had a little daughter.
When her mother washed her face
it looked very rosy,
but when she washed mine it did not look so.

In vain, I tried washing to make my face
the same colour as little Mary,
I began to be mortified
at the difference in our complexions.

31.
I remained here till the summer of the year 1757,
when my master was appointed first lieutenant
of his majesty's ship the *Roebuck*.

We set out for England in a sloop
bound for London.
As we were coming up the Nore where the *Roebuck* lay,
a man of war's boat came along-side to press our people.
Each man ran to hide himself.
I was very frightened
and hid under a hencoop.

The press gang came on board
swords drawn, searching about,
pulling people out by force
putting them into the boat.

At last I was found and held up by the heels
while they all made sport.
I was roaring and crying out most lustily.

The mate, my conductor, came to my assistance
did all he could to pacify me till we saw the boat go off.
Soon, to our joy, my master came on board
and brought us to the ship.

32.

When I first came among the Europeans,
apprehensions and alarms had taken
such strong possession of me.
I began now to pass to an opposite extreme.

My surprise began to diminish
as my knowledge increased.
I was so far from being afraid
of anything new which I saw,

I remained in the ship a considerable time
and visited a variety of places.
   Twice in Holland.
   Leith in Scotland.
   Thence to the Orkneys
   (where I was surprised to see scarcely any night).

We were frequently chasing vessels
off the coast of France.
I had learned many ship manoeuvres
and was made several times to fire the guns.

I began to long for an engagement.

The Seven Years' War

THE SEVEN YEARS' WAR (1756–1763) WAS A GLOBAL CONFLICT
that involved several European nations, including rivals Britain and France. At the conclusion of the war, Britain defeated France and established itself as an empire, taking control of the Atlantic Coast of North America, key areas of the Caribbean, and India.

As the enslaved servant of an officer, Olaudah Equiano had a front-row seat to intense battles of the war, including the Battle of Quiberon Bay and the siege of Louisbourg. As the British navy became the most powerful in the world, Equiano became a skilled sailor. At the time, 6 to 8 percent of British sailors were Black, which was greater than the percentage of Black people in England's overall population. Racial prejudice was also diminished in the close quarters of a ship, where sailors depended on one another for their lives. For Olaudah Equiano, life as an enslaved sailor meant traveling the world, gaining valuable nautical skills, and learning to read and write. After the war, he moved from working aboard military ships to working on merchant ships, which allowed him to earn money and eventually purchase his freedom.

33.

Dick and I were on board
the *Savage* sloop of war for weeks
when my master sent us to London,
the place long desired to see.
A Mr. Guerin and his two sisters
(very amiable ladies)
took great care of me.
I had the chilblains and
could not stand for several months.
I was sent to St. George's Hospital
and grew so ill doctors wanted to cut off my leg.
I said I would rather die.
Happily, I recovered without the operation.
Then the small-pox broke out.
Again confined
I thought myself particularly unfortunate
but soon recovered again.

34.

My master was promoted
first lieutenant of the *Preston*,
a man of war of fifty guns.
Dick and I were sent on board.
Soon we went to Holland to bring the body of
the Late Duke of Cumberland to England.

Next my master was appointed a lieutenant
on board the *Royal George*—
the largest ship I had ever seen.
I was surprised at the number of people,

men, women, and children of every denomination,
the largeness of the guns,
shops and stalls with every kind
of good, and people crying their different commodities
about the ship as in a town.
To me it appeared a little world.

We did not stay long here before the crew of the *Royal George*
was turned over to Vice-Admiral Boscawen.
My master got an appointment on the *Namur*,
which was fitting up with a large fleet for an expedition.
I hoped to soon be gratified with a sea fight.

35.
At last this mighty fleet weighed anchor and sailed.
We steered for America but contrary winds
drove us to Tenerife, its noted peak
of prodigious height resembling a sugar loaf.
I was filled with wonder.

We remained in sight of this island some days,
then proceeded for America
into a very commodious harbour
called St. George in Halifax.
We had fish in plenty
and all other fresh provisions.

Joined by different transport ships with soldiers,
we sailed for Cape Breton in Nova Scotia
with good and gallant General Wolfe on board.

His affability made him highly esteemed
and beloved by all the men.

36.
Summer of 1758.

We arrived in Cape Breton
to attack Louisbourgh.

I was gratified to see an encounter
between our men and the enemy.

The French on shore disputed our landing
but were at last driven from their trenches.

Our troops pursued them
and many were killed on both sides.
Our land forces laid siege to the town
while the French men of war
were blocked by the fleet.
I saw ships set on fire
by the shells from the batteries.

Captain George Balfour
liked me so much
that he often asked my master to let him have me,
but he would not part with me
nor I him.

37.

At last Louisbourgh was taken
and the English came into the harbour.
Great joy, for now I had more liberty
and often went on shore.

We had the most beautiful procession on the water.
All the admirals and captains full dressed.
Barges well ornamented with pendants.

The Vice-admiral went on shore
followed by the other officers in order of seniority
to take possession of the town and fort.

The French governor and his lady came on board to dine.
Our ships were dressed with colours of all kinds
and this, with the firing of guns,
formed a most grand and magnificent spectacle.

38.

As soon as everything was settled,
we sailed for England. It was now winter.
One evening during our passage home,
about dusk, seven sail stood off shore.
Both fleets began to mingle.
The other fleet hoisted their French ensigns
and gave us a broadside.

Nothing could create greater surprise
and confusion among us than this.
The wind was high, the sea rough,

not a single gun ready to be fired
at any of the French ships.

Immediately the ships were made ready for fighting.
We gave chase pursuing them
       all night
            all day
                all night.

The sea grew smoother. The wind lulled.
We chased, but the next day
they were out of sight.
We saw no more of them and soon made land.
Once safe, the Admiral went to London.

My master and I followed with a press gang
for we wanted some hands.

Press Gangs

STARTING IN THE FOURTEENTH CENTURY, A SIGNIFICANT PORTION OF THE sailors in the British Royal Navy were recruited by force. This was known as impressment. "Press gangs" could board other ships or go into towns and make able-bodied men join their ranks. During times of war, the risk of being impressed was especially high; an estimated one-third to one-half of sailors in the royal fleet were forced to join. Of course, when sailors were taken against their will in the first place, there was a higher chance they would desert. The rough treatment of sailors, including the possibility of being violently forced into service by a press gang, was discussed alongside the issue of slavery. The parallels may have made European society more sympathetic to enslaved Africans' experience. In the mid-1800s impressment ended, after many people had adopted the language of antislavery activists and called for the "abolition" of the practice.

CHAPTER FOUR
To See Fresh Wonders

39.

Now three and four years
since I first came to England,
a great part spent at sea.
I began to consider myself happily situated,
treated well, and a stranger to terror.

My attachment and gratitude to my master were great.
I never felt half the alarm at any number of dangers
that I was filled with at first sight of Europeans.
That fear, the effect of my ignorance,
wore away as I began to know them.

I could now speak English tolerably well, and
I understood everything said.
I felt easy, relished their society and manners and
had the strong desire to imitate them.

I no longer looked upon them as spirits.
I was almost an Englishman.

40.

I had long wished to read and write
and took every opportunity to gain instruction.
When I went to London with my master,
he sent me to wait upon the Guerin ladies
who sent me to school.

While I was attending these ladies,
their servants told me I could not go to heaven
unless I was baptized.
I had a faint idea of a future
and pressed the eldest Miss Guerin
to be baptized.

My master refused.
   She insisted.
      He complied with her request.

I was baptized at St. Margaret's church
February 1759
by my present name.

41.

The *Namur* again got ready for sea,
my master ordered on board.
I was to leave my school master,
whom I liked very much.
I parted from the Miss Guerins
with uneasiness and regret.
They often used to teach me to read
and instruct me in religion.
I parted with reluctance.

We were destined for the Mediterranean
In the spring of 1759 we got to Gibraltar.
While here, I was often on shore.

42.
I had told several people the story
of my kidnapping,
of my sister,
of being separated,
of my anxiety for her fate,
of my sorrow at never having met her again.

One day, someone told me
that he knew where my sister was
that he would bring me to her.
My heart leaped for joy.
Improbable as this story was,
I believed it
and agreed to go with him.
He conducted me to a black young woman
so like my sister at first sight
I really thought it was.

Upon talking, I found her to be of another nation
and was quickly undeceived.

43.
While we lay here, the *Preston* came in.
My master told me I should now see Dick,
who had gone when she sailed for Turkey.
I rejoiced and ran to inquire.

I learned from the boat's crew
that my friend was dead.
They brought his things to my master
who gave them to me.

Inexpressible sorrow!
A memorial for the dear youth,
whom I loved and grieved for
as a brother.

44.
After lying in Gibraltar,
we sailed up the Mediterranean.
One night we were overtaken
by a terrible gale of wind.
The sea ran so high.
The ship rolled so much.

After a short time we came to Barcelona,
a Spanish sea-port remarkable for its silk.
Soldiers were stationed along the shore.
Natives sold us fruits of all kinds
much cheaper than in England.
They brought wine in hog and sheep skins.

The Spanish officers treated our officers
with politeness and attention.
Some came to visit my master,
would mount me on horses
so I could not fall
and set them off at full gallop.

My imperfect horsemanship
no small entertainment.

45.
We returned to cruising
for French ships.
One day alarmed
by signals, a cry:
the French fleet was out.

It is impossible to describe the
              noise
                      hurry
              confusion
of making ready for fighting.

We set out in the dark.
At daylight we saw seven sail of ships
and immediately chased them
until about four o' clock in the evening
when our ships came up with them.

The engagement now commenced
with great fury on both sides,
and we continued for some time.
I was frequently stunned
with the thundering of great guns.

My station during the engagement
was on the middle deck.
Here I was witness to the dreadful fate

of many of my companions,
who in the twinkling of an eye
were dashed in p i e c e s
and launched into eternity.

I escaped unhurt,
though the shot and splinters
flew thick about me.
My master was wounded
and carried down to the surgeon.
I was much alarmed
and wished to assist him, but
I dared not leave my post.
I expected every minute to be my last,
our men fell so thick about me.

With the reflection that there was
a time allotted for me to die
as well as be born,
I instantly cast off all fear of death.
If I survived the battle,
I had the hope of relating
the dangers I had escaped
when I returned to London.

46.
At last, the French line, broken.
Victory, immediately proclaimed!
Loud huzzas and acclamations.

We took three prizes, and
the rest of the French took flight.
Two large French ships endeavoring to escape
ran ashore on the coast of Portugal.
We set fire to them both.

About midnight I saw one blow up,
a dreadful explosion.
I never beheld a more awful scene.
The midnight seemed turned into day by the blaze
the noise louder and more terrible
than thunder.

Our own ship was torn to pieces.
Once refitted, we steered for England.

47.

When my master recovered,
the Admiral appointed him Captain
of the *Ætna*, a fire ship.
I liked this small ship,
became a captain's steward,
was happy and treated well
by all on board.

I had leisure to improve myself
in reading and writing
which I learned while on the *Namur* as
there was a school on board.

Then the King died,
which caused our ship to be stationed
in the Isle of Wight,
till the beginning of sixty-one.
I was on shore all about this delightful island
and found the inhabitants very civil.

While in a field belonging to a gentleman
a black boy about my own size
ran to meet me with haste,
caught hold of me in his arms
as if I had been his brother
though we had never seen each other before.

We talked together some time.
After, he took me to his master's house,
where I was treated kindly.
We were happy seeing each other
till March 1761 when our ship
had orders for another expedition.

We sailed once more in quest of fame,
I longed for new adventures and fresh wonders.

48.
The 5th of April.

We had on board, a gunner whose name was John Mondle,
a man of indifferent morals.
This man's cabin was between decks,
over where I lay.

Terrified with a dream,
he woke in so great a fright
he could not rest in bed
nor remain in his cabin.

He went on deck extremely agitated,
immediately told of his dream.
He told of the agonies in his mind.
He had seen many awful things.
He had been warned to repent
His time was short and, alarmed,
he was determined to alter his life.

Some of his shipmates who heard laughed.
He vowed never to drink strong liquor and
began to read the Scriptures, hoping to find some relief.
Soon after, he laid himself down to sleep.

I heard people in the waist cry out:
The Lord have mercy upon us! We are all lost!

Mr. Mondle, hearing the cries, ran out of his cabin.
We were instantly struck by the *Lynne*,
a forty-gun ship.
She struck our ship with her cutwater
right in the middle of his bed and cabin.
There was not a bit of wood to be seen
where Mr. Mondle's cabin stood.
So near being killed,
some of the splinters tore his face.

Had he not been alarmed
Mr. Mondle must have perished from this accident.

Our ship was in such shocking condition
we all thought she would go down.
Using every possible means,
she was kept together.

Every thing uncommon made a full impression on my mind.
Every extraordinary escape or deliverance
(either of myself or others)
I looked upon as a sign.
I thought I could plainly trace the hand of God
without whose permission a sparrow cannot fall.
I began to raise my fear from man to him alone
and to call daily on his holy name.

The 8th of April.

We had refitted our ship.
All things were in readiness for attack.
The troops were ordered to disembark.
My master, now junior captain, commanded the landing.
The French were drawn up on shore
to oppose the landing of our men.

Most of our men were cut off after fighting with great bravery.
General Crawford and others, taken prisoner.
Our lieutenant killed.

The 21st of April.

We renewed our efforts to land the men,
fired at the French batteries
till our soldiers made a safe landing,
immediately attacked the French,
and proceeded to besiege the citadel.
My master was ordered on shore
to superintend the materials necessary,
in which service I mostly attended him.

While there, I went about, and one day
my curiosity almost cost me my life.
I wanted to see the mode of charging the mortars
and letting off the shells,
and went to an English battery a few yards from the citadel
completely seeing the whole operation,
a great risk from both English shells that burst
and from those of the French.
One of the largest bursted
within nine or ten yards of me.
The earth was torn
and threw great quantities of stones and dirt.

Perilous circumstances!
I attempted to return the nearest way I could find.
I observed at a little distance a French horse,
took some cord, made a kind of bridle,
and put it round the horse's head.
The tame beast quietly suffered me.

On the horse's back,
I began to kick and beat him
and try every means to make him go quick,
but I could not drive him out of a slow pace.
While creeping along,
still within reach of the enemy's shot,
a servant on an English horse appeared.
I immediately stopped and, crying, begged him help me.
He began to lash my horse so severely with a large whip
that he set off full speed with me towards the sea.

Quite unable to hold or manage him,
I went along till I came to a craggy precipice.
I could not stop my horse,
my mind filled with my deplorable fate.
I thought I had better throw myself off
and fortunately escaped unhurt.
I made my way to the ship,
determined not to be so fool-hardy again.

49.
We continued to besiege the citadel
till June, when it surrendered.
After the taking of this island
our ships went to block a French fleet
from June till February.
Sometimes we would attack the French.
Once or twice the French attacked us
throwing shells with their bomb-vessels.

Our ship was sent
to St. Sebastian in Spain,
to Bayonne in France,
to Belle-Isle,
to Portsmouth
to Guernsey
to Portsmouth.

When our ship arrived
we heard talk about peace
and to our great joy,
in the beginning of December,
we had orders to go to London with our ship
to be paid off.

We received this news with loud huzzas,
and every demonstration of gladness.
I was not without my share of joy.
I thought now of nothing but
being freed and working for myself
being freed and getting money
being freed and getting a good education
being freed
being able to read
being able to write
being freed.

50.

On the *Ætna* was Daniel Queen,
a man about forty years of age
and very well educated.
He dressed and attended the captain.

He instructed me in many things:
taught me to shave and dress hair
and also to read the Bible,
explaining many passages to me
which I did not comprehend.
He was like a father to me.
Indeed I almost loved him
with the affection of a son.

He would say
he and I never should part
that when our ship was paid off,
as I was as free as himself or any other man on board,
he would instruct me in his business
by which I might gain a livelihood.

This gave me new life.
My heart burned within me.
Though my master had not promised me freedom
I was told he had no right to detain me,
had always treated me with the greatest kindness.
never suffered me to deceive him or tell lies.
From all this tenderness, I never supposed
he would detain me
any longer than I wished.

51.

In pursuance of our orders
we sailed for the Thames
and arrived the 10th of December
where we cast anchor
just as it was high water.

The ship was up about half an hour,
when my master ordered the barge to be manned.

All in an instant,
with no reason to suspect,
he forced me into the barge
saying I was going to leave him,
but he would take care I should not.

I was so struck with unexpectedness
for some time I could not reply.
I asked to go for my books and clothes,
but he swore I should not move,
and if I did he would cut my throat.

I began to collect myself.
Plucking up courage, I told him I was free,
by law, he could not serve me so.

This enraged him more.
He continued to swear
and sprung himself into the barge from the ship
to the astonishment and sorrow of all on board.

The tide, unluckily for me, had just turned.
We went down the river with it.

He resolved to put me on
the first vessel he could.
We came alongside a ship,
the *Charming Sally* sailed by Captain James Doran
going away the next tide for the West Indies.
My master went on board.
Soon I was sent to the cabin.

Captain Doran asked me if I knew him.
I answered that I did not.
Then, said he *you are now my slave.*
I told him my master could not sell me
to him nor any one else.
Did not your master buy you? he said.

I confessed he did.
But I have served him many years.
He has taken all my wages during the war.
Besides, I have been baptized.
By the laws of the land
no man has a right to sell me.

Captain Doran said I talked too much English
and if I did not be quiet,
he had a method to make me.

I was too convinced of his power over me
to doubt what he said.

52.

Recollections of my former sufferings
in the slave-ship made me shudder.
I filled with resentment.
My master took with him
the only coat I had with me
and said *If your prize-money had been 10,000 pounds
I had a right to it all, and would have taken it.*

I had nine guineas
scraped together.
I hid it that instant
still hoping by some means or other
I should make my escape to shore.

My master concluded his bargain with the captain,
came out of the cabin, got into the boat, and put off.
I followed with aching eyes as long as I could.
When they were out of sight
I threw myself on the deck,
heart ready to burst
with sorrow and anguish.

CHAPTER FIVE
Curse the Tide

53.
At the moment I expected
all my toils to end
I was plunged in a new slavery.

I wept for some time.
My mind now began to think
I must have done something
to displease the Lord
that he punished me so severely.

In time, my grief
began to subside
and my thoughts reflected calm.

I considered that trials and disappointments
sometimes teach wisdom and resignation.
God had shadowed me with wings of mercy
his invisible but powerful hand
brought me the way I knew not.

These reflections gave me little comfort.
I rose from the deck,
dejection and sorrow in my countenance,
yet with some faint hope
for my deliverance.

54.
The 30th of December.

To my inexpressible anguish,
we made a signal for sailing.
The ships got up their anchors,
and our ship got under way.

Tumultuous emotions agitated my soul.
I was a prisoner without hope,
my eyes upon the land
in a state of unutterable grief.

The fleet sailed on
and in one day's time
I lost sight
of the wished-for land.

I was ready to curse the tide
ready to curse the ship
ready to be relieved from the horrors I felt.

55.

The 13th of February, 1763.

From the mast-head: Montserrat
a land of bondage.
Fresh horror ran through my frame
and chilled me to the heart.

My former slavery now rose
in dreadful review:
misery
       stripes
              chains.

I called upon God's thunder,
his avenging power,
to direct the stroke of death to me
rather than permit me to become a slave
and be sold from lord to lord.

I now knew what it was to work hard.
I was made to unload and load the ship.
So long used to an European climate
I felt the scorching sun painful.
The dashing surf tossed the boat and
I was day by day mangled and torn.

56.

About the middle of May,
Captain Doran sent for me one morning,
my fate was determined.

The captain told me if he were to stay in the West Indies
he would keep me himself,
but he could not take me to London
for he was sure that that I would leave.

He told me he had instead
got me the very best master
with whom I should be happy
as if I were in England.

Mr. King (my new master) said
I should be well off with him.
He did not live in the West Indies but Philadelphia.

He bought me on account of
my good character
and good behavior
and he would put me to school for a clerk.
This relieved my mind and left me more at ease.

57.
Mr. King, a Quaker and a merchant,
a most amiable disposition,
very charitable and humane.
If any of his slaves behaved amiss,
he did not beat them but parted with them.

This made them afraid
as he treated his slaves better
than any on the island and
was more faithfully served by in return.

He asked me what I could do
and did not mean to treat
me as a common slave.

I knew something of seamanship
could shave and dress hair pretty well
could refine wines
could write.
I understood arithmetic as far as the Rule of Three.

He asked if I knew of gauging.
On answering that I did not,
he said one of his clerks should teach me.

Mr. King dealt in all manner of merchandize
kept from one to six clerks
had many vessels of different sizes
to go about the islands and collect
rum, sugar, and other goods.

I rowed the boat, slaved at the oars
from one hour to sixteen in the twenty-four.
This hard work in the sugar seasons was
my constant employment.

58.
There was scarcely any part
of Mr. King's business or household affairs
in which I was not engaged.

I worked likewise on board of different vessels of his.
I often supplied the place of a clerk
in receiving and delivering cargoes to the ships,
in tending stores,
in delivering goods.
Besides this, I shaved and dressed my master
and took care of his horse.

By these means I became very useful
and saved him a hundred pounds a year.
as I was of more advantage to him
than any of his clerks.
I have sometimes heard it asserted
that a negro cannot earn his cost.
Nothing can be further from the truth.

Throughout the West Indies
nine tenths of the mechanics are negro slaves.
So too the
      Coopers
        Carpenters
          Masons
            Smiths
              Fishermen.

If it be true,
why do the planters and merchants pay
such a price for slaves?

Sugar Production

BECAUSE OLAUDAH EQUIANO WAS LITERATE AND POSSESSED
other valuable skills, he was able to avoid working in the sugarcane fields. Sugar was the primary crop grown in the Caribbean.
Because it was very lucrative, the vast majority of enslaved people on British islands such as Jamaica worked in sugar production. French colonies were also major producers of sugar. Europeans used it in their coffee and tea as well as to make jams and
chocolate.

Growing and processing sugar was a brutal business. It takes
fourteen to eighteen months for sugarcane to grow and become
ripe. Enslaved workers used sharp machetes to cut and harvest it.

CUTTING AND CARRYING THE CANE

The Spanish brought sugarcane to the Caribbean in 1493. By the mid-1700s,
sugarcane was the most popular and most lucrative import in Britain.

Mills crushed the cane and extracted its juice, which was then boiled to produce syrupy brown molasses and sugar. Molasses could be distilled to make rum. Each step of the process was exhausting. The mills and boiling houses were hot and dangerous. Hands and arms could be caught in machinery. During the harvest season, enslaved people worked constantly. The sugar had to be processed day and night. Instead of providing enslaved workers with livable conditions and reasonable hours, owners preferred to work them as hard as possible, even if it meant they became ill or died. The enslavers would simply replace their workers when a new batch of captives was brought to the slave markets.

Sugar became Britain's largest import in the eighteenth century. Many people grew wealthy from the profits of its cultivation. People in Britain understood the connection between their sugar and slavery. When Parliament rejected an abolition bill in 1791, hundreds of thousands of British people responded by participating in a sugar boycott. This effort was led by women, who used their control over the food in their homes as political power. Some people stopped sweetening their tea altogether, while others switched to using sugar from India.

59.

I was often witness to cruelties of every kind
exercised on my unhappy fellow slaves.

It was very common in the islands
for men to purchase slaves
(though they have not plantations themselves)
in order to let them out for so much by the day.
They give their slaves what scanty allowance they choose.
I had fifteen pence sterling per day to live on—
considerably more than was allowed to others
Some were given no allowance at all.

It was very common in the islands
For men to leave management of their estates to
overseers, persons of the worst character,
human butchers who cut and mangle slaves in a shocking manner.
No regard to pregnant women
the least attention to the lodging of field negroes.
This neglect certainly causes
a decrease in births and lives.

It was very common in the islands
for slaves to be branded
with the initials of their master's name
and a load of heavy iron hooks hung about their necks.
The iron muzzle and thumb-screws applied for the slightest faults.
I have seen a negro beaten, his bones broken,
for letting a pot boil over.

It was very common in the islands.

60.

Pray reader,
Is not the slave trade entirely a war
with the heart of man?

I have often seen slaves put into scales
weighed then sold
three pence | six pence | nine pence a pound.
My master used to sell by the lump.

It was not uncommon
to see husbands taken from their wives,
wives taken from their husbands,
and children from their parents,
sent off to other islands
and wherever else their merciless lords chose,
to see each other never more during life!

At these partings my heart has bled,
the friends of the departed at the water side
with sighs and tears,
                        eyes fixed on the vessel
                                    till it went out of sight.

61.

In all the different islands in which I have been
(no less than fifteen)
the treatment of the slaves was nearly the same.

The slave-trade has a tendency
to debauch men's minds,
to harden them to every feeling of humanity!

Dealers are not born worse than other men.
It corrupts human kindness.
Had the pursuits of those men been different
they might have been
as generous, tender-hearted, and just
as they are unfeeling, rapacious, and cruel.

Surely this traffic cannot be good,
which violates that first natural right of mankind:
equality and independence.

It raises the owner to a state far above.
It depresses the slave below.

Are slaves more useful being humbled
to the condition of brutes
than if suffered to enjoy
the privileges of men?

When you make men slaves,
you deprive them of half their virtue,
you compel them to live with you
in a state of war.

Are ye not struck with shame and mortification?
Are ye not hourly in dread of an insurrection?

By changing and treating your slaves as men,
every cause of fear would be banished.
They would be faithful and honest,
intelligent and vigorous.

Peace, prosperity, and happiness would attend you.

Rebellion in the Caribbean

PLANTATION OWNERS IN THE CARIBBEAN WERE TERRIFIED OF THE possibility of rebellion. On most Caribbean islands, the population of enslaved people was larger than the population of plantation owners and overseers. One reason for the brutal style of slavery in the West Indies was to try to prevent a violent uprising. In a vicious cycle, the enslavers' own brutality increased their fear that enslaved people might seek violent revenge for this inhumane treatment.

In the late 1700s, the people of France overthrew their monarchy and established a democracy. They adopted the Declaration of the Rights of Man and of the Citizen and wrote a new constitution. Many people of African descent in the Caribbean took note of the French Revolution and its messages about human rights. Soon afterward, the largest slave rebellion in the history of the region took place on Saint-Domingue, a French colony located on

Born into slavery on Saint-Domingue, Toussaint L'Ouverture received his manumission sometime before the revolution.

the western part of the island of Hispaniola in the area that is known as Haiti. An army of rebellious enslaved people led by Toussaint L'Ouverture violently attacked the plantations and their inhabitants. They burned everything in sight. L'Ouverture's army was relentless and fought for months until most of the white people either fled or were killed. At that point, France abolished slavery throughout its West Indian empire. The British army tried to take over the island, but they too were defeated by Toussaint L'Ouverture.

England would eventually make a trade agreement with L'Ouverture on the condition that he would not spread ideas about rebellion to those enslaved on neighboring British islands, such as Jamaica and Barbados. Nevertheless, there were revolts in both of those colonies. While European gentlemen across the sea debated the future of slavery, enslaved people in the Caribbean were breaking their chains by force. Their willingness to fight for freedom helped wear down the will of slavery's defenders. The potential for continued deadly uprisings became a highly compelling reason to end slavery.

CHAPTER SIX
I Determined to Make Every Exertion

62.
1763.
Kind providence.

Captain Thomas Farmer,
an Englishman
commanded one of my master's vessels and
had taken a liking to me.

Many times he begged my master
let me go with him
for sailors were scarce in the island.
My master reluctantly let me go
but told him to take care I did not run away
for if I did, he would make him pay.

I was very happy at this proposal.
Immediately I thought I might stand a chance
to get a little money
or possibly make my escape.

The captain liked me very much,
and I was his right-hand man.
I became so useful the captain would tell my master
I was better than any three white men he had.
I did all I could to deserve his favour.

63.

After sailing for some time
I tried my luck as a merchant.
I had very little to begin with:
one single half bit,
equal to three pence in England.

On St. Eustatia, a Dutch island,
I bought a glass tumbler with my half bit.
When I came to Montserrat
I sold it for a whole bit, or sixpence.

Luckily, we made several trips to St. Eustatia.
Finding my tumbler profitable,
I bought two more.
I sold them for two bits
equal to a shilling sterling.

With these two bits
four more glasses,
which I sold for four bits on our return.

Next two glasses and
a three pint jug of gin,
all sold for a dollar
in the space of a month.

Thus was I going about the islands
four years trading.
I blessed the Lord that I was so rich.

64.
Daily exposed to new hardships in the West Indies,
every part of the world seemed, in comparison,
a paradise.

My mind replete with thoughts of being freed,
although I could see no means
or hope to obtain my freedom.

What-ever fate had determined
must come to pass.
If it were my lot to be freed
nothing could prevent me.

On the other hand,
if it were my fate not to be freed
I never should be so.

I anxiously looked up
with prayers for my liberty.
At the same time, I used every
honest means to obtain it.
In time I became master of a few pounds,
which my friendly captain knew very well.

I foresaw my well-being
and future hopes of freedom
depended on this man.
and therefore continued with him.
From my great attention to his orders and his business,
I gained him credit.

On "Benevolent Slave Masters"

OLAUDAH EQUIANO OFTEN SPEAKS ABOUT INSTANCES WHERE various people who enslave or oversee him are "kind." He differentiates between white Europeans who used him "well" and those who used him "ill." He expresses gratitude toward his enslavers and even thinks of some as father figures or mentors. However, this affection was undermined by the enslavers continuing to hold legal and physical power. On a day-to-day basis, a master who treated him well meant that Equiano experienced more physical and mental safety as well as the agency to move about, gain useful skills, and make the money he would use to free himself. From Equiano's perspective, a "kind" master meant a more likely path to freedom. Equiano strategically tried to stay close to those who might help him reach his goal of liberation.

When Olaudah Equiano's book was published, emancipation for all enslaved people was not a popular idea. Abolitionists were working to end the slave trade, but they were not yet able to convince British society or the British government to end slavery altogether. In the meantime, Equiano wanted to pressure enslavers to treat people more humanely, and that might be another reason he praised the ones he considered kind.

From a modern perspective, an enslaver who treated people humanely was still wrong to build wealth by purchasing human beings, imprisoning them against their will, and forcing them to work. Even the most "benevolent" enslaver deprived people of basic human rights. Regardless of the intent of any individuals, the system of slavery was brutal, unjust, and a violation of human rights.

65.

While I went on resisting oppression
with thoughts of freedom,
my life hung daily in suspense,
as I could not swim.

Throughout the West Indies, the surfs are violent,
their howling rage
their devouring fury
can strike and toss a boat
maiming several on board.

Once in the Grenada islands,
I and eight others
were pulling a large boat,
when a surf struck us and drove the boat
among some trees.

Once in Montserrat
I was very near being drowned.
The jacket I had on kept me above water
while I called on a man near me
and told him I could not swim.
He made haste as I was sinking,
caught hold and brought me to sounding.

Once when going in a large canoe
a single surf tossed us
an amazing distance from the water.
Most of us were very bruised.

I often said no other place
under the heavens as this.
I longed to leave it,
and daily wished
to go to Philadelphia, my master's promise.

66.
While we lay in this place
a very cruel thing
which filled me with horror,
happened on our sloop.

A very clever and decent free mulatto man
who sailed a long time with us
had a free woman for his wife,
by whom he had a child.
She was living on shore and all were very happy.
Everyone knew this young man was free.
No one had ever claimed him as their property.

As might too often overcomes right
a Bermudas captain came on board
and seeing the mulatto man
told him that he was not free
told him he had orders from his master
to bring him to Bermudas.

Although the man showed a certificate
of being born free in St. Kitts,
he was taken forcibly without any hearing on shore
or to even see his wife or child.

He was carried away,
doomed never more in this world
to see them again.

This barbarity was frequent,
free men villainously held in bondage.
These things opened my mind to a new scene of horror
of which I had been before a stranger:
I had thought only slavery dreadful,
but the state of a free negro appeared even worse,
for they live in constant alarm for their liberty.

Is it surprising that slaves,
when mildly treated,
should prefer the misery of slavery
to such a mockery of freedom?

I was now completely disgusted
and thought I never should be free
until I had left the West Indies.

The Abolition Movement in England

AT THE TIME THAT HE WROTE HIS BOOK, EQUIANO AND OTHERS IN THE abolition movement in England were specifically working to end the slave trade. They wanted to establish a new economic system with African societies that traded goods rather than human beings. Slavery was so embedded in the British economic and political systems that many were afraid to ask for complete emancipation of all enslaved people throughout the British colonies.

British people benefited greatly from the slave trade, and many did not think it was wrong. Powerful shipping companies and rich plantation owners were determined to keep the industry going to protect their profits. Even powerful government entities, like the Church of England and the British army, bought and owned enslaved people. The Royal African Company, started by English monarchs King Charles II and King James II, traded more enslaved Africans than any other British organization.

Laws protecting workers of any race were not well established, so many white English workers were mainly concerned with their own working conditions and treatment. It was still common for white people to serve as indentured servants and to be pressed into military service against their will. One of the arguments against the slave trade was actually the poor treatment, and consequent high death rate, of white sailors: one in five perished. Still, many individuals, as well as groups such as the Quakers, recognized enslaving other people was immoral and believed that ending the slave trade was a necessary first step. They organized meetings, distributed thousands of pamphlets, and encouraged boycotts of goods produced with enslaved labor. Between 1787 and 1792, 1.5 million people in Britain signed anti-slavery petitions.

67.
I determined
to obtain my freedom
and return to Old England.

I thought a knowledge
or navigation might be of use.
If I understood navigation,
I might attempt my escape in our sloop—
one of the swiftest sailing vessels in the West Indies—
at no loss for hands to join me.

I had the mate of our vessel teach me
for which I paid him twenty-four dollars.
However, my progress was reduced
by the constancy of our work.

Had I wished to run away,
opportunities frequently presented themselves
particularly one time soon after this.

When at the island of Guadeloupe
a large fleet of merchantmen bound for Old France—
seamen being very scarce—
gave fifteen to twenty pounds a man for the run.
Our mate and all the white sailors left
and went on the French ships.
They swore to protect me if I would go with them,
and I believe I could have got safe to Europe.

However, my master was kind.
Remembering "honesty is the best policy"
I would not attempt to leave
And suffered them: *go without me.*

68.
This fidelity
turned to my advantage
when I did least think it.

As my master fitted out his vessel for Philadelphia,
in the year 1765, he sent for me to his house.
There I found him and the captain together.

He heard I meant to run away
when I got to Philadelphia.
I was astonished.

Therefore, I must sell you.
You cost me no less than forty pounds,
and it will not do to lose so much.
You are valuable, and I can get
one hundred guineas for you.

I told my master I did not say I would run away.
I appealed to the captain, whether he saw sign
of my making attempt to run.

Did I not come on board on time?
When all our men left and went on the French fleet,
and advised me go with them, I did not.

To my joy, the captain confirmed
every syllable I said.
He never found I made the smallest attempt.

This speech of the captain
like life to the dead
gladdened my poor heart beyond measure.

My master then gave me a silver coin, rum, and sugar
that by carrying things to different places
I might have money to purchase my freedom.

My master would let me have it
for forty pounds sterling,
the same price he gave for me.

69.
A change indeed.
In the same hour to feel
        the most exquisite pain
and in the turn of a moment
        the fullest joy.

When I left the room
I immediately went
        (or rather flew)
to the vessel,
which being loaded, we sailed
and arrived safe at the elegant town
of Philadelphia.

I soon sold my goods here pretty well.
In this charming place I found everything
plentiful and cheap.

70.
We sailed for Montserrat,
once more to encounter the raging surfs.
We arrived safe and discharged our cargo.
Soon after, we took slaves on board
for St. Eustatia and then to Georgia.

I always exerted myself and did double work
and from overworking myself while we were at Georgia
I caught a fever and was very ill near dying.
Dr. Brady attended me, and
I was restored again to health.

Soon after, the vessel loaded,
we set off for Montserrat.
When we were safe arrived we took in
         (as usual)
some of the poor oppressed
natives of Africa and other negroes.
We set off again for Georgia and Charlestown.

We arrived at Georgia, landed part of our cargo,
and proceeded to Charlestown with the remainder.
While there I saw the town illuminated.
         guns and bonfires
         other demonstrations of joy shewn:
the repeal of the Stamp Act.

CHAPTER SEVEN
Nearer My Freedom

71.
Every day now brought me
nearer my freedom,
I was impatient to purchase it.

In the beginning of 1766,
my master bought another sloop, the *Nancy*,
the largest I had ever seen.
Our Captain had his choice of three,
and I was pleased he chose the largest.
I had more room and could carry with me
a larger quantity of goods.
With these views, I sailed for Philadelphia.

We arrived safe and in good time,
I sold my goods to the Quakers.
They appeared to be honest people,
and never attempted to impose.
I therefore chose to deal with them
in preference to any others.

My traffic had succeeded so well
that I thought when we arrived at Montserrat,
I should have enough to purchase my freedom.

72.
When we once more arrived safe in Montserrat,
I had sold my venture and had
about forty-seven pounds.

How I should proceed in offering
my master the money for my freedom?
I consulted my true and honest friend, the Captain.

He told me to come on a certain morning
when he and my master would be at breakfast.

That morning I went with my money in my hand
and many fears in my heart.
I prayed my master to be as good as his offer
when he promised me my freedom
as soon as I could purchase it.

This speech seemed to confound him.
He began to recoil,
and my heart that instant sunk.

> *What?* said he. *Give you your freedom?*
> *Why, where did you get the money?*
> *Have you got forty pounds sterling?*

Yes, sir I answered.

    How did you get it?

I told him *Very honestly.*

    The Captain said he knew
    I got the money with much industry,
    and that I was particularly careful.

My master said
that I got money much faster than he did,
that he would not have made me the promise
if he had thought I should have got money so soon.

    Come, come said my Captain,
    clapping my master on the back,
    You must let him have his freedom.
    You have laid your money out very well
    received good interest,
    now here is the principal at last.
    Come, Robert, take the money.

My master then told me to go
to the Secretary at the Register Office
and get my manumission drawn up.

These words were like a voice from heaven.
All my trepidation turned into unutterable bliss.

I most reverently bowed myself with gratitude,
unable to express my feelings
but by the overflowing of my eyes.

I left the room in order to obey
my master's joyful mandate.

73.
The Register congratulated me
and told me he would draw up
my manumission for half price.

I thanked him for his kindness, and paid him.
I hastened to my master to get him to sign it,
that I might be fully released.

He signed the manumission that day.

Before night, I
who had been a slave in the morning—
trembling at the will of another—
had become my own master,
completely free.

I thought this
was the happiest day
I had ever experienced.

74.

As my manumission
expresses the absolute power and dominion
one man claims over his fellow,
I shall present it at full length:

*Montserrat.—To all men unto whom these presents
shall come: I Robert King, of the parish of St. Anthony in
the said island, merchant, send greeting: Know ye, that I
the aforesaid Robert King, for and in consideration of the
sum of seventy pounds current money of the said island, to
me in hand paid, and to the intent that a negro man-slave,
named Gustavus Vassa, shall and may become free, have
manumitted, emancipated, enfranchised, and set free, and
by these presents do manumit, emancipate, enfranchise, and
set free, the aforesaid negro man-slave, named Gustavus
Vassa, for ever, hereby giving, granting, and releasing unto
him, the said Gustavus Vassa, all right, title, dominion,
sovereignty, and property, which, as lord and master over
the aforesaid Gustavus Vassa, I had, or now I have, or by
any means whatsever I may or can hereafter possibly have
over him the aforesaid negro, for ever. In witness whereof I
the above-said Robert King have unto these presents set my
hand and seal, this tenth day of July, in the year of our Lord
one thousand seven hundred and sixty-six.*

ROBERT KING.
*Signed, sealed, and delivered in the presence of Terrylegay,
Montserrat. Registered the within manumission at full
length, this eleventh day of July, 1766, in liber D.
TERRYLEGAY, Register.*

75.

Fair as well as black people
immediately styled me by Freeman,
the most desirable appellation in the world

At dances,
my superfine blue clothes
made no indifferent appearance.
Females who formerly stood aloof
began to relax.
But my heart was still fixed on London
where I hoped to be.

My captain and late master said to me
We hope you won't leave us, but that you
will still be with the vessels.
Gratitude bowed me, struggling between inclination and duty.

Though my wish was London,
I obediently answered I would not leave them.
I entered on board as a sailor
at thirty-six shillings per month.

I determined to make a voyage or two to please
my patrons, but the year following
I would see
England once more
and surprise my old master, Captain Pascal.
I pleased myself thinking of what he would say
when he saw what the Lord had done in so short a time.

I embarked on the *Nancy*
in my free African state.

76.
As we set sail, the captain and mate complained of sickness.
As we proceeded, they both grew worse.
This was November,
and we had not been long at sea
before we met with northerly gales
and rough seas.

We attended to the pumps
every half or three quarters of an hour.
The captain and mate came on deck
as they were able,
which was seldom
for they declined so fast.

The care of the vessel rested on me
to direct her by my former experience.
The captain was now sorry
he had not taught me navigation.

His illness increased so much that
he was obliged to keep his bed.
When he found the symptoms of death
approaching, he called me by my name.
While I was expressing my
affection and sorrow by his bedside,
he expired without saying another word.

We committed his body to the deep.

77.

The care of the vessel took all my time
and attention entirely.
I steered for Antigua, the nearest island to us.
In nine or ten days,
to our great joy, we made this island.
Next we came to Montserrat.

Many were surprised when they heard
I conducted the sloop into port.
I was called Captain. As high a title
as any free man in this place possessed.
This was quite flattering.
I was offered (and refused) the command
of a gentleman's sloop

When the death of the captain became known,
it was regretted for he was
a man universally respected.
I did not know, till he was gone,
the strength of my regard.
Had he died but five months before,
I should not have obtained my freedom.

Part Two

CHAPTER EIGHT
If I Should Still Be Saved

78.

As I had now lost my great benefactor and friend, my captain,
I had little inducement to remain longer in the West Indies,
except my gratitude to Mr. King.

I thought I had done well bringing back his vessel
and delivering his cargo to satisfaction.
I began to think of leaving this part of the world,
(of which I had been long tired)
and returning to England
(where my heart had always been)
but Mr. King pressed me to stay.

I found myself unable to refuse
and consented to another voyage.

On the 30th of January 1767 we steered for Georgia.
Our new captain boasted of his skill in navigating,
steering a new course several points more west
than we ever did before.

This appeared to me extraordinary, and at night
I dreamt the ship wrecked amidst surfs and rocks,
that I was the means of saving everyone on board.

The night following,
I dreamed the very same dream.

79.

The next evening being my watch, I went up on deck.
At half after one in the morning, the man at the helm
saw something that the sea washed against.

He immediately called to me that there was a grampus
and desired me look at it. I stood
and observed it for some time.

I saw the sea wash up against it
again and again, I said it was not a fish
but a rock.

Being certain of this, I went to the captain,
told him the danger we were in and
to come upon deck immediately.

The wind abated a little.
The vessel carried sideways by the current
towards the rock. Still the captain did not appear.

The noise of the breakers all around us,
I was exceedingly alarmed and lost all patience.
I ran down to him again.

The breakers are round us, and the vessel almost on the rock.
We called all hands immediately. The surf
foaming round us, a dreadful noise.

The moment we let the anchor go the vessel struck
the rocks. A single heave of the swells,
the sloop was pierced!

A scene of horror I never conceived before.
No mind was ever like mine: so replete with inventions
and confused with schemes how we might be saved.

How to escape death I knew not.
All my sins stared me in the face. I determined
if I should still be saved, I would never swear again.

In the midst of my distress, calling to mind
the many mercies God had shown me
gave me some small hope he might still help.

80.
The captain ordered the hatches
nailed down on the more than
twenty slaves in the hold, all of whom
would have perished if he had been obeyed.
When he desired to nail down the hatches,
I desired them to stop.

The captain said it must be done.
Every one would get into the small boat,
and we should be drowned,
for it would not have carried above ten at most.

I could no longer restrain
and told him he deserved drowning
for not knowing how to navigate.
I believe the people would have tossed him
overboard if I had given them the hint.

The hatches were not nailed down.

None of us could leave the vessel. On account
of the dark, we knew not where to go
and were convinced that the boat could not
survive the surf.

We would remain on the dry part of the vessel
and trust God till daylight.

81.
Our boat had a piece out of her
two feet long, and we had no materials
to mend her. Necessity being the
mother of invention, I took some leather,
nailed it to the broken part,
plastered it over with tallow-grease.

With anxiety we watched for daylight.
At last it appeared to our longing eyes.
The dreadful swell began to subside.
We discovered a small island,
about five or six miles off, but there was
not enough water for our boat to go over the reefs.

All of us had to get out to drag and lift it,
with labour and fatigue.
We could not avoid having our legs
cut and torn with the rocks.

Only four people would work
with me at the oars,
three black men and a Dutch Creole sailor.
Not one of the white men
did anything to preserve their lives.
Our labour intolerably severe,
the skin entirely stript off my hands.

We continued to toil and strain
till we had brought all safe to shore.
Of thirty-two, we lost not one.

My dream returned with all its force.
Our danger the same I had dreamt
fulfilled in every part.

82.
This key
a Bahama island
a mile in circumference
a white sandy beach
some very large birds called flamingoes
as large as men.
To our joy and wonder,
they took flight.

There were turtles
and several fish in such abundance
that we caught them without bait.
We made tents to lodge in,
with sails we brought from the ship.
Determined to repair our shattered boat,
we began to think how we might put to sea.

Eleven days, the boat ready,
the captain and myself with five more
set off towards New Providence
with two musket loads of gun-powder,
three gallons of rum,
four gallons of water,
some salt beef,
biscuits.

In this manner we proceeded to sea.

83.
On the second day we came to an island called Abbico.
Much in want of water, we hauled the boat ashore.

The place was a thick wood. When it was dark,
we made a fire for fear of wild beasts.

Unwelcome night! We took turns to watch, found little rest
and waited with impatience for morning.

As soon as light appeared we set off again.
Now weakened, our terror became great.

We expected nothing but death.
We tried to fish, but could not
and began to despair.

In the midst of our murmuring, the captain cried out
A sail! A sail! A sail!

We steered after it.
To our unspeakable joy, we saw it was a vessel.

Our spirits revived, we made towards her
with all the speed imaginable.

We came near a little sloop,
a wrecker, employed to look after wrecks,
quite full from a whaling schooner wrecked two days before.

We begged them to go to our key directly
because our people were in want of water.

In two days we arrived
to the inexpressible joy of those we had left behind.

84.
After sailing for days
we got safe to New Providence.

The inhabitants here were very kind
There were some free black people
who were very happy.
We passed our time together

pleasantly with the melodious sound of the catguts,
under the lime and lemon trees.
Many friends encouraged me to stay there
but I declined.

My heart was fixed on England.

85.
Captain Phillips hired a sloop
to carry him and some of the slaves
he could not sell to Georgia.
I agreed to go with him,
and we sailed about four in the morning
and in seven days' time arrived safe.

We went up to Savannah
and I went to a friend's house to lodge
whose name was Mosa, a Black man.
We were very happy at meeting each other.

After supper, we had a light on, and
about that time the watch patrol came by
and knocked at the door.
We opened it and they came in and sat down,
and drank punch with us.

They knew I was a free man and
told me I must go to the watch-house with them.
After our kindness to them, this surprised me.
I asked them, *Why?*

They said all negroes
who had light after nine o'clock
were to be taken into custody
and either pay or be flogged.
As the man of the house was not free,
and had his master to protect him,
they did not take him.

I told them I was free,
that I just arrived from Providence,
that we were not making any noise,
that I was not a stranger,
that I was very well known there.

What will you do with me?

That you shall see, replied they,
but you must go to the watch-house with us.

I was at a loss whether they meant
to get money from me or not.
Seeing that nothing would pacify them,
I went to the watch-house,
where I remained the night.

Early the next morning they
were going to lay violent hands on me
when one of them (more humane than the rest)
said that as I was a free man
they could not justify stripping me by law.

I immediately sent for Doctor Brady,
known to be an honest and worthy man.
On his coming to my assistance,
the rogues let me go.

86.
This was not the only incident
I met with in this place.

I stayed in Savannah,
anxiously trying to get to Montserrat to Mr. King,
my old master, then to take a final farewell
of the American quarter of the globe.
I met with a sloop called the *Speedwell*
bound to Martinico, a French island,
with a cargo of rice.

I shipped myself on board,
bade adieu to Georgia,
and sailed.

87.
After an absence of six months
I finally arrived in Montserrat.
I saw my friends with gladness,
increased by the dangers I had escaped.
I told Mr. King I intended to go to London that season
that I had come to visit him before my departure.

The good man expressed a great deal of affection for me
and sorrow I should leave him,

advised me to stay
insisting I was respected and
might do very well,
might have land and slaves of my own.

I thanked him but declined.
I requested a certificate of my behaviour while in his service
which he readily gave me:

*Gustavus Vassa, my slave for three years behaved himself well
and discharged his duty with honesty.*

88.
I bade Montserrat farewell

bade adieu to the angry, howling, dashing surfs
bade adieu to oppressions
bade adieu to the sound of the cruel whip
bade adieu to all other dreadful instruments of torture.

I have never had my feet on it since.

With a light heart, I embarked for London,
on board a ship called the *Andromache*
exceedingly glad to see myself
steering the course I had long wished for.

We had a prosperous voyage and
at the end of seven weeks arrived at Cherry-Garden.
My eyes were once more gratified with a sight of London
after being absent from it four years.

I received my wages and
entered upon a scene quite new to me
full of hope.

89.
My first thoughts
were to look for my former friends.
The first were the Miss Guerins.
I went in quest of those kind ladies,
and with some difficulty and perseverance,
I found them at Greenwich.
They were agreeably surprised to see me.
I told them my history, at which they
wondered.

Their cousin Capt. Pascal,
visited frequently,
and four or five days after, I met him.
He appeared surprised,
and asked me how I came back?

In a ship.

He replied dryly,
I suppose you did not walk back to London on the water.

He did not seem sorry
for his behaviour to me.
I told him that he had used me ill
after I had been faithful to him
so many years.

Without saying more,
he turned about and went away.

A few days after, we met again
at Miss Guerin's house
and I asked him for my prize-money.

He said there was none due me
for he had right to it all.

I told him I was informed otherwise.

In a bantering tone, he bade me
to commence a lawsuit against him.
There are lawyers enough
that will take the cause in hand, and you had better try it.

I told him then that I would,
which enraged him.
However, out of regard to the ladies,
I never made any farther demand of my right.

90.
Some time afterwards these friendly ladies
asked me:
What did I meant to do with myself?
And how they could assist me?
I thanked them, and said, if they pleased,
I would be their servant.
They answered me very politely
that they were sorry but

it did not suit them to take me as their servant.
They could recommend me to some person
who would teach me a business,
whereby I might earn my living.
What business should I like to learn?
I said, hair-dressing.

They then promised to assist me and soon after
recommended me to one Captain O'Hara,
who treated me with much kindness,
and procured a master hair-dresser
with whom he placed me.

I was with this man from September
till the February following.

91.
We had a neighbour who taught French horn.
I was charmed with it
and he agreed to teach me.
Accordingly, he began to instruct me,
and I learned all three parts.
I took great delight in this instrument.
I did not like to be idle,
and it filled my vacant hours.

Rev. Mr. Gregory, who kept an academy
and an evening-school, lived in the same court
and agreed to improve me in arithmetic.

In February 1768, I hired myself to Dr. Charles Irving,
celebrated for his successful experiments
making sea water fresh.
I had plenty of hairdressing to improve.
This gentleman was excellent
and allowed me to attend school in the evenings,
a great blessing.

I used my diligence and attention
to improve the opportunity.

Apprenticeships

DURING THE EIGHTEENTH CENTURY, AN APPRENTICESHIP WITH A skilled worker, or a "master" of the craft, was the most common way to receive training in many lines of work. It was a formal relationship, bound with signed documents and ruled by laws. Apprenticeships often began when workers were young. They might live with the skilled worker and earn their keep while learning specialized skills in trades such as tailoring, hat-making, leather processing, metal working, carpentry, or shipbuilding.

People of African descent who ended up in England found few job opportunities in trades, as they were in direct competition with white workers of lower classes. Further, they were often too old for apprenticeships to learn new trades. Most Black Britons worked in domestic service and held various roles in households alongside white servants.

After purchasing his freedom in his early twenties, Olaudah Equiano had the ability to pay a master hairdresser to train him to cut and style hair, shave beards, and make wigs. Gaining these skills allowed Equiano to make money doing something other than sailing. It also brought him into contact with powerful individuals including Dr. Charles Irving, who employed Equiano for some time.

92.

I soon found my wages
(two thirds less than I ever had in my life)
would not be sufficient to continue
to pay necessary expenses.
My thirty-seven guineas had worn away to one.

I thought to try the sea again
in quest of more money.
I also had a desire to see Turkey,
and I determined to gratify it.
In May of 1768, I told the doctor
my wish.
He made no opposition,
and we parted.

The same day I went to the city
and heard of a gentleman
who had a ship going to Italy and Turkey.
He wanted a man who could dress hair and
hired me immediately.
I was overjoyed
and went immediately on his ship.

93.

Voyage to Italy aboard the *Delaware*:
charmed with the rich beauty of
Villa Franca
Nice
Leghorn

Struck with the
elegant buildings
extraordinary good wines
and rich fruits.

94.
When we left Italy, we sailed
among the Archipelago islands,
and to Smyrna in Turkey,
a very ancient city
stone houses
have graves adjoining,
and sometimes appear as churchyards.

Provisions plentiful
grapes, pomegranates, and other fruits
the richest and largest I ever tasted.

The natives are well looking and
treated me always with great civility.
I believe they are fond of black people
and several gave me
invitations to stay among them.

I was surprised to see how
Greeks are kept under the Turks,
as the negroes in the West Indies
are by white people.

I was astonished not seeing women
in any shops

and rarely in the streets.
When I did, they were covered with a veil
from head to foot
so that I could not see their faces
except when out of curiosity they
uncovered them to look at me,
which sometimes they did.

During our stay here—
about five months—
I liked the place and the Turks.
Our ship richly loaded with silk
and other articles,
we sailed for England.

95.
May 1769.

After Turkey
Oporto in Portugal
where we arrived at carnival.
On our arrival, none of us dared to go
till the Inquisition searched
for everything illegal on board,
especially bibles.
Any person in whose custody
a concealed bible was found
was imprisoned and flogged
and sent into slavery for ten years.

The town is pretty
with all kinds of provisions.

I saw many magnificent sights, but
could not gain admittance to their churches
without the necessary sprinkling of holy water at my entrance.
I complied with this ceremony
from curiosity (and a wish to be holy)
but its virtues were lost on me.

Our ship having taken in a load
sailed for London
and arrived in July.

96.
September 1769.

Our next voyage was to the Mediterranean
Genoa, one of the finest cities I ever saw.
Noble edifices of beautiful marble with fountains before them,
made a most noble appearance.
Rich and magnificent churches were
curiously adorned both inside and out.

But all this grandeur was in my eyes
disgraced by the condition of the galley slaves,
truly piteous and wretched.

After, we sailed to Naples,
a charming city, remarkably clean
the bay the most beautiful I ever saw.

Extraordinary grand operas on Sunday nights
are attended by their majesties.
I too, like these great ones, went to those sights.

There was an eruption of Mount Vesuvius,
of which I had a perfect view.
It was extremely awful and we were so near
that ashes were thick on our deck.

After we had transacted our business at Naples,
we sailed once more for Smyrna,
The merchants here travel in caravans
with hundreds of camels
laden with different goods.
The people of these caravans are quite brown.
They brought with them
a great quantity of locusts,
which are sweet, pleasant to the palate
and in shape resembling French beans.
Each kind of good is sold in a street by itself.
I always found the Turks very honest in their dealings.
They let no Christians into their mosques or churches,
for which I was very sorry.
I was fond of seeing the different modes
of worship of the people wherever I went.

The plague broke out while we were in Smyrna,
and we stopped taking goods till it was over.
The ship was then richly laden,
and we sailed for England.
When we arrived my noble captain, the ship, and I
all separated.

CHAPTER NINE
A Roving Disposition

97.
April 1771.

Aboard *The Grenada Planter*
Captain William Robertson
to Madeira
to Barbados
to Grenadas
goods to sell

Former West India customers
a white islander man
no intention of paying
threatened me and another
Although free Negroes
no remedy

Luckily three white sailors
also in search
stripped him

He begged for mercy
offered some small allowance
ran into the bushes

Bon Voyage

98.
Being still of a roving disposition
desirous of seeing
as many different parts of the world as I could,
I shipped myself as steward
on board a fine large ship,
the *Jamaica*.

Captain David Watt
sailed from England in December 1771
for Jamaica,
a large island and well peopled—
a vast number of negroes.

In Kingston I was surprised
to see the number of Africans
assembled together on Sundays,
each different nation of Africa meet and dance
after the manner of their own country.
They retain native customs:
bury their dead,
put victuals, pipes, and tobacco
in the grave with the corpse
in the same manner as in Africa.

I saw many cruel punishments inflicted
on the slaves in the short time I stayed.
I was present when a poor fellow was tied
and kept hanging by the wrists
some distance from the ground,
some half hundred weights
fixed to his ankles,
in which posture he was flogged
unmercifully.

99.
On return to London,
I waited on my old master, Dr. Irving,
who made me an offer
of his service again.
Being tired of the sea,
I gladly accepted.

I was very happy and
we were daily employed
in reducing old Neptune's dominions
by purifying the briny element
and making it fresh.

Thus I went till May 1773,
when roused by the sound of fame
to seek new adventures
and to find towards the north pole
a passage to India.

An expedition on board the *Race Horse* was now fitting out
to explore a north-east passage.
My master anxious for this adventure
prepared everything for our voyage
and I attended him.

On the 4th of June we sailed
towards the pole,
the ship so filled
that there was little room on board.

On the 20th of June we began to use
Dr. Irving's distillery and
purified twenty-six to forty gallons a day.
The water distilled perfectly pure
and tasted free from salt.

It became extremely cold and we saw
many high and curious mountains of ice.
In Greenland, I was surprised
to see the sun did not set.

A great number of very large whales
used to come close to our ship
and blow water to a very great height
in the air.

We killed many different animals,
including nine bears, all very fat.
I thought them coarse eating,
but some relished them.

One morning about the ship
we had vast quantities of sea horses
which neighed exactly
like any other horses.
We fired harpoon guns
but could not get any.

We saw one continued plain of smooth
unbroken ice bounded only by the horizon.
The reflection of the sun
from the ice, gave the clouds
a most beautiful appearance.

Sunshine and constant daylight
gave cheerfulness and novelty
to the whole of this striking,
grand, uncommon scene.

100.
We remained until the 1st of August
when the two ships got completely fastened in the ice.
Our situation dreadful and alarming,
in great apprehension of having the ships
squeezed to pieces.

The officers now held a council
in order to save our lives.
It was determined
we should endeavour to escape
by dragging our boats on the ice
towards the sea,
farther off than any of us thought.

Filled with despair
we had very little prospect of escaping with life.

We sawed some ice about the ships
to keep it from hurting them and kept them
in a kind of pond.

We then began to drag the boats
towards the sea.
After two or three days,
we made very little progress
and really began to give up.
                    Our deplorable condition!
                    Our lamentable appearance!
The fears of death hourly upon me
and exceedingly doubtful of a happy eternity
if I should die in it.

On the eleventh day,
the wind changed,
the weather immediately became mild,
and the ice broke towards the sea!

With all our might we shoved the ships
into open water and made sail.
This seemed a reprieve from death.
We proceeded till we got to the open water again,
to infinite joy and gladness of heart.

Out of danger,
we refitted.

The 19th of August
we sailed from this uninhabited extremity of the world,
where inhospitable climate
affords neither food nor shelter,
not a tree or shrub of any kind grows
amongst its barren rocks.
One desolate, expanded waste of ice,
which even the constant sun
for six months in the year cannot penetrate or dissolve.

We sailed for London and
thus ended our Arctic voyage
having been absent four months,
in imminent hazard of our lives.
We explored much farther
than any had ventured before.
We fully proved the impracticability
of finding a passage that way to India.

Dr. Irving and the North Pole Expedition

DR. CHARLES IRVING, A NAVAL SURGEON AND INVENTOR FROM London, created a machine that could remove the salt from seawater to make it drinkable. Irving first hired Equiano as a hairdresser and then to help with the machine on a well-known Arctic expedition. The voyage was led by a future baron, and Equiano's traveling companions also included future admiral and war hero Horatio Nelson. While the expedition was ultimately unsuccessful in its mission to find a passage to India, it was an adventure that took Equiano to the brink of the world (and death), then back.

HMS *Racehorse* and HMS *Carcass* in the ice during their 1773 voyage. Irving and Equiano were employed on the *Racehorse*.

CHAPTER TEN
I Rejoiced in Spirit

101.
Our voyage to the North Pole ended,
I returned to London with Doctor Irving.
I began to reflect on the dangers I had escaped
which made a lasting impression,
and by the grace of God,
proved afterwards a mercy to me.
It reflected deeply on my eternal state,
determined to work out my own salvation.

I left Doctor Irving, the purifier of waters,
and lodged in Coventry-court, Haymarket,
where I was much concerned about the salvation of my soul.

I enjoyed the French horn
and dressing hair for some months.
Experiencing the dishonesty of many,
I determined to set out for Turkey to end my days.

It was now early spring 1774.

102.

I sought for a master,
and found Captain John Hughes,
commander of *Anglicania*,
sitting out in the river Thames and bound to Smyrna in Turkey.
I shipped myself with him as a steward.

I recommended to him a clever black man,
John Annis, as a cook, who
had formerly lived many years
with Mr. William Kirkpatrick,
a gentleman of the island of St. Kitts
from whom he parted by consent.

Mr. Kirkpatrick came to our ship at Union Stairs
on Easter Monday, April the fourth,
with two boats and six men,
having learned the man was on board.
They tied and forcibly took him from the ship,
in the presence of the crew and the chief mate,
who had detained him.
I believe that this was a combined piece of business
as they did not in the least assist to recover him.

I proved the only friend
who attempted to regain his liberty,
having known the want of liberty myself.

I got knowledge of the ship in which he was
but unluckily she had sailed the first tide.

My intention was to immediately
to apprehend Mr. Kirkpatrick
who was about setting off for Scotland
and, having obtained a habeas corpus for him,
and got a tipstaff to go with me
to St. Paul's churchyard where he lived.

He, suspecting something,
set a watch.
I whitened my face that they might not know me,
and this had its desired effect.

He did not go out that night
and next morning my tipstaff,
who got admittance into the house,
was to conduct him to a judge
according to the writ.
When he came, his plea was
he did not have the body in custody.
He was admitted to bail.

I proceeded immediately to philanthropist
Granville Sharp, Esq.
who received me with utmost kindness
and gave me instruction.

I left him in hope
that I should gain the unhappy man his liberty,
with gratitude towards Mr. Sharp for his kindness.

Alas! my attorney proved unfaithful
took my money,
lost me months employ,
and did not do the least good.

When John Annis arrived at St. Kitts,
he was staked to the ground,
cut and flogged,
and afterwards loaded cruelly with irons about his neck.

I had two moving letters from him.
Some London families saw him in St. Kitts
in the same state in which he remained
till kind death released him out of the hands
of his tyrants.

Granville Sharp

IN 1772, A MAJOR COURT CASE CHANGED THE WAY SLAVERY worked in England. A well-known white lawyer and abolition activist named Granville Sharp represented James Somerset, a Black man who escaped from his enslaver when he was brought to England from the West Indies. Judge Lord Mansfield ruled that if an enslaver brought an enslaved person from the Americas to England, they could not force the enslaved person to return to the Americas. The ruling allowed Somerset to remain a free person and had an impact on other enslaved people because it was widely (and falsely) believed that Mansfield had actually outlawed slavery. After the ruling, if an enslaved person could escape their enslaver, they were less likely to be pursued. Many in the Black British community sought Sharp out when they needed legal help, feeling that he believed in the humanity of Black people and in their right to be free.

Equiano read and appreciated Sharp's books, and Equiano informed him of the Zong massacre, which Sharp then widely publicized. Sharp also supported Equiano by subscribing to the editions of his narrative as they were published and was one of the last people to visit him on his deathbed.

103.
Determined to go to Turkey.
Resolved never more to return to England.
Prevented by my captain, Mr. Hughes, and others.

All appeared to be against me,

Thus I continued in heaviness.
until a dissenting minister invited me
to a love-feast at his chapel that evening.
I accepted,
and thanked him.

When the hour came I went.
and was much astonished to see the place filled with people,
no signs of eating and drinking.
There were many ministers in the company.
They began by giving out hymns.
Their language and singing did harmonize,
and between the singing
the minister engaged in prayer.

I knew not what to make of this sight,
having never seen anything of the kind
before now.

Some of the guests began to speak their experience,
much was said by every speaker
of the providence of God
and his unspeakable mercies.

This I knew in a great measure
and could most heartily join them.

Some persons produced baskets of buns,
which they distributed,
and each person communicated with his neighbour,
and sipped water which they handed to all present.
This kind of Christian fellowship I had never seen,
nor ever thought of seeing on earth.
It reminded me of what I had read
in scripture of the primitive Christians,
who loved each other and broke bread.

Thus I went on happily for near two months.

104.
Out of employ,
nor likely to get a situation suitable,
obliged me once more to sea.

Engaged as steward of the *Hope*
with Captain. Richard Strange,
bound from London to Cadiz in Spain.

Cadiz is strong,
commands a fine prospect,
and is very rich.
The Spanish galleons frequent that port,
and some arrived whilst we were there.
I began to think I had lived a moral life,
to believe I had divine favour.

It was given to me at that time
to know what it was to be born again.
The word of God?
Sweet to my taste!
Sweeter than honey.

The burden of sin,
the gaping jaws of hell,
and the fears of death,
that weighed me down before
now lost their horror.
I longed to tell of
the wonders of
God's love towards me.

We remained at Cadiz until our ship got laden
and arrived in London
the month following.

I went and saw some old friends,
who were glad
the wonderful change wrought in me.
I was received into church fellowship
and rejoiced in spirit.

Christianity and Slavery

OLAUDAH EQUIANO DOCUMENTED A LIFE OF SPIRITUAL GROWTH AS he became more and more committed to his Christian beliefs. At the time, it was commonly believed that a Black person who had been baptized could not be enslaved because Christians did not enslave other Christians. Many Black British people converted to Christianity in order to support their quests for freedom. Some, like Equiano, became actively interested in evangelical work that would draw more people to their faith. Much of Equiano's memoir is dedicated to describing his faith and transformation through Christianity.

At the time, the most popular and powerful church in England was the Church of England, also known as the Anglican Church. It had been established in the sixteenth century when King Henry VIII separated from the Catholic Church and its leader, the pope. Nearby countries, such as Italy, Spain, and France, were still heavily influenced by the Catholic Church.

There were also groups of people called Dissenters who were trying to separate from the Anglican Church. They included early Methodists, Baptists, Lutherans, and Quakers. The "dissenter" churches were particularly popular with both free and enslaved Black people, as they often supported abolition and preached that salvation was available to anyone no matter their station in life. In particular, an early sect of evangelical Methodists called the Countess of Huntingdon's Connexion attracted the attention of Black intellectuals and writers, including Equiano, Phillis Wheatley, and John Marrant.

Still, the most powerful churches were not strong proponents of abolition. Neither the Catholic Church nor the Church of England effectively used their power to end slavery. In fact, the Church of England's missionary organization owned a large plantation on Barbados named Codrington where several hundred people were enslaved.

On an individual level, white Christians disagreed about the relationship between their faith and slavery. Some Christians thought that because the Bible did not say slavery was wrong, they could continue enslaving Africans. They felt they were doing a good thing by introducing enslaved people to European culture and religion. Other Christians said it was hypocritical to be both a Christian and a supporter of slavery. Equiano ultimately stopped participating in sailing and other slave-trade-related activities because he wanted to live a life more in line with his Christian values of doing good work, which included becoming a voice for abolition.

CHAPTER ELEVEN
A Mind for a New Adventure

105.
I was happy once more
amongst my friends,
till my old friend Doctor Irving
bought a remarkable fine sloop, about 150 tons,
for a new adventure
cultivating a plantation at Jamaica
and the Musquito Shore.
He asked me to go with him.
as he would trust me in preference to any one.

By the advice of my friends,
I accepted.
I hoped to bring some poor sinner
to Jesus Christ.

Before I embarked,
I found with the Doctor
four Musquito Indians,

who were chiefs in their own country,
brought here by English traders for some selfish ends.

One of them, the Musquito king's son,
about eighteen years of age,
was baptized George.
They were going back
at the government's expense,
having been in England about twelve months,
during which they learned to speak English.

We embarked in November 1775,
on the *Morning Star* under Captain David Miller
and sailed for Jamaica.
I took all the pains to instruct
the Indian prince in the doctrines of Christianity
and he was attentive.
I taught him in eleven days all the letters
and he could even put two or three together and spell.

Some began to ask him
whether I had converted him to Christianity
laughed
and made jest.
I rebuked them as much as I could,
but this treatment caused the prince to halt
between two opinions.
He would not learn any more, which
grieved me very much.

106.

In January
we arrived at Jamaica.
One Sunday I took
Prince George to church.
When we came out, we saw all kinds of people
half a mile down to the water
buying and selling all kinds of commodities.

I went with the Doctor on board a Guinea-man
to purchase slaves to carry with us
and cultivate a plantation
and chose all my own countrymen.

On the twelfth of February
we sailed from Jamaica,
on the eighteenth
arrived at the Musquito shore.

All our Indian guests went ashore
and were met by the Musquito king.

We never saw one of them after.

The Mosquito (Musquito or Miskitu) Coast

SOON AFTER RETURNING FROM THE ARCTIC, DR. IRVING AND HIS business associates decided to establish a cotton and castor oil plantation on the Mosquito Coast, an area of the coast of present-day Honduras and Nicaragua that was home to the Miskitu people. There the castor plant that produces castor oil, a useful ingredient for making soap, grew wild. The British also wanted a stronger foothold to ward off the Spanish, whom they had been fighting for control of the area, and in 1740, Britain and the Miskitu king signed a treaty that created an alliance allowing British settlements in the region in exchange for military protection from Spain. Dr. Irving's ship, the *Morning Star*, was stolen by the Spanish coast guard.

Equiano was hired as an overseer. His job was to help manage and communicate with the enslaved Igbo people who were bought to work on the plantation. Although he saw himself as a compassionate overseer, he was still participating in slavery.

Britain would withdraw from the area in 1787, leaving it in control of Spain.

107.

We sailed south of the shore
to Cape Gracias a Dios.
There was a large lagoon
which received
two or three rivers
and abounded in fish and land tortoise.

Some of the native Indians seemed pleased
we were to dwell amongst them
and took us to view the land
to choose a place
to make a plantation.

We fixed on a spot
near a river, in a rich soil.
We began to clear away the woods
and plant different kinds of vegetables,
which grow quick.

Our vessel went north
to Black River to trade.
There, a Spanish guarda costa
took her, a great embarrassment.
However, we went on with the land.

We used to make fires
every night all around us
to keep off wild beasts,
which set to hideous roaring
as soon as it was dark.

Our habitat in the woods,
saw different animals,
none ever hurt us—
except poisonous snakes
which the Doctor cured.

The Indians were exceedingly
fond of the Doctor
and came from all quarters to our dwelling.
Some who lived fifty
or sixty miles above our river,
this side of the South Sea,
brought us silver
in exchange for our goods.

108.

We could get
from our neighbour Indians:
turtle oil,
      shells,
            little silk grass,
                  some provisions.

They would not work
for us, except fishing.
A few times they assisted
to cut trees down
to build us houses,
which they did exactly
like Africans: the joint labour
of men, women, and children.

The country hot,
we lived under an open shed
without a door or lock,
yet we slept safe and
never lost a thing.

This surprised us
and we used to say
if we were to lie in that manner
in Europe we should have
our throats cut the first night.

The Indian governor goes
about the province or district,
settles all the differences
among the people, like the judge,
a number of men with him
as attendants and assistants,
and is treated with great respect.

He took care to give us notice
before he came,
by sending his stick as a token
for rum, sugar, and gunpowder,
which we did not refuse sending.
At the same time
we prepared
to receive his honour.

The natives boast
of having never been
conquered by
the Spaniards.

109.
The rainy season came
about the end of May,
and continued
till August.

The rivers overflowed
our provisions washed away
I thought this a judgment upon us
for working on Sundays.

Though attached to the doctor,
I often wished to leave
and sail for Europe.
It was disagreeable for me
to stay any longer.

Living in this mode was irksome to me.
About the middle of June I took courage enough
to ask him for my discharge.

At first, he was unwilling
to grant my request,
but I gave so many reasons for it
he consented to my going at last.

Happy he consented,
I got everything ready,
and hired some Indians
with a large canoe to carry me off.

When they heard of my leaving them,
the slaves, my countrymen,
were very sorry
as I had always treated them
with care and affection.

110.

On the 18th of June, accompanied by the doctor,
I left that spot of the world
and went south along the river.
There I found a sloop going to Jamaica
Having agreed for my passage,
the doctor and I parted,
shedding tears on both sides.

The vessel sailed till night,
when she stopped in a lagoon.
During the night a schooner came
in want of hands.
The owner of the sloop
asked me to go in the schooner as a sailor
and said he would give me wages.

I thanked him but said I wanted to go to Jamaica.

He immediately changed his tone
swore at me
and cursed the master
that sold me my freedom.
desired me to go in the schooner
or else I should not leave the sloop as a freeman.
I begged to be put on shore again,
but he swore that I should not.
I said I could not have expected
this amongst Christians.
Incensed,
he swore he would sell me.

I asked what right he had to sell me.
Without another word, he made his people
tie ropes round my ankles,
to each wrist,
and another round my body,
and hoisted me up
without letting my feet touch or rest
upon anything.

Thus I hung,
without any crime committed
without judge or jury
merely because I was free.
I was in great pain
and cried and begged for mercy,
but in vain.

My tyrant, in a great rage,
brought a musket out, loaded it
before me and the crew and swore
that he would shoot me if I cried more.

I had no alternative,
remained silent.
Not one white man on board
said a word on my behalf.

I hung
from ten/eleven o'clock at night
till about one in the morning
when—my cruel abuser fast asleep—
I begged his slaves
to slack the rope round my body,
that my feet might rest on something.
They did at the risk of being cruelly used by their master.

When the vessel was getting under way,
I once more cried
begged to be released.
Being in the way of hoisting the sails,
they released me.

When I was let down, I spoke to Mr. Cox,
a carpenter, who desired a young man
put me ashore in a canoe.
I got hastily into the canoe and set off for my life.

111.

On shore I was directed to an Indian chief,
the Musquito admiral
who had once been at our dwelling.
He was glad to see me, refreshed me,
and I had a hammock to sleep in.

I told the admiral I wanted to go to the next port
to get a vessel to carry me to Jamaica.
He agreed and sent five able Indians
with a large canoe to carry my things,
and we set off the next morning.

The sea was so high
that the canoe was often
near being filled with water.
We were obliged to go ashore
and drag across land.
Two nights in the swamps,
swarmed with mosquito flies.

This tiresome journey of land and water
ended on the third day.
I got on board a sloop
commanded by one Captain Jenning
who told me he was expecting daily to sail for Jamaica.

Having agreed to work my passage,
I went and was not many days on board
when to my sorrow and disappointment
(though used to such tricks)

we went to the south along the Musquito shore,
instead of steering for Jamaica.

I was to cut mahogany wood
as we coasted along the shore
and load the vessel before she sailed.

I did not know how to help myself
among these deceivers.
I thought patience the only remedy,
and even that was forced.
There was much hard work
and little on board to eat.

112.
I was on board sixteen days, and
during our coasting
we came upon a smaller sloop
the *Indian Queen* commanded by John Baker
an Englishman
trading turtle shells and silver
along the shore.

He wanted hands very much, and
understanding I was a free man
he told me if he could get one or two,
he would sail immediately for Jamaica.
He promised me forty-five shillings sterling a month.
Much better than cutting wood for nothing.

July 10th I got my things
and went on the *Indian Queen*.
To my great mortification
this vessel went south
trading along the coast
instead of to Jamaica as promised.
Worst, the captain was cruel and bloody-minded
a horrid blasphemer.

One day he got a barrel of gunpowder on deck
and swore that he would blow up himself and me.
There was another vessel in sight
(which he supposed was Spaniard),
and he was afraid of falling into their hands.
I placed myself between him and the powder, resolved.

It was actually an English sloop,
and they soon came to an anchor.
To my no small surprise,
Doctor Irving was on board
on his way to Jamaica.

I learned that after I had left the estate,
a white overseer had taken my place.
This man beat and cut the slaves,
and the consequence was
that everyone got into a large canoe
to escape, but not knowing where to go
or how to manage the canoe,
they were all drowned.

The doctor was now returning to Jamaica
to purchase more slaves
and stock his plantation again.

113.
On the 14th of October the *Indian Queen*
arrived at Kingston in Jamaica.
I demanded my wages.
Captain Baker refused to give me one farthing
though it was the hardest-earned money
I ever worked for in my life.

Doctor Irving did all he could
to help me get my money.
Every magistrate in Kingston (there were nine)
refused to do anything
and said my oath could not be admitted
against a white man.

Such oppressions made me seek
to get off the island as fast as I could.

In November
I found a ship bound
for England, which I embarked
having taken a last farewell of Doctor Irving.

When I left Jamaica, he was employed refining sugars.
Some months after my arrival in England,
I learned with sorrow

my friend was dead,
having eaten some poisoned fish.

January 1777, we arrived at Plymouth.
I was happy once more
to tread upon English ground.
I went to London
with thanks to God for past mercies.

CHAPTER TWELVE

Go Ye and Do Likewise

114.
Such were the various scenes
which I was a witness to
until the year 1777.
Since that period, my life
has been more uniform.
I therefore hasten to the conclusion
of a narrative, which I fear
the reader may already think tedious.

I suffered so many impositions
in different parts of the world
that I was determined
not to return to seafaring
at least for some time.

I continued, therefore
in service
until 1784.

In spring, I thought of visiting the old ocean.
I embarked as steward
on a fine new ship called the *London*,
and sailed for New York.
This city is large and well-built,
and abounds with provisions of all kinds.
We returned to London in January 1785.

When she was ready again for another voyage,
I sailed with the captain again in March 1785 for Philadelphia,
very glad to see this old town once more.
My pleasure increased
in seeing the Quakers
freeing and easing the burthens
of many oppressed African brethren.

I rejoiced when one
took me to see a free-school
for black people,
whose minds are cultivated
and made useful members of the community.
Does not the success of this practice say loudly
in the language of scripture—
Go ye and do likewise?

The Black Community in England

DURING THE EARLY EIGHTEENTH CENTURY, THE POPULATION OF people of African descent living in England was small and included both enslaved and free Black people. Some Black Britons had escaped from enslavers when they were visiting from the Americas. Others were the children of mixed-race relationships. Some were students from West Africa whose fathers were chiefs. A large portion were sailors whose merchant or navy ships had let them off in an English port. Most worked in the service industry as domestic help. Through his writing and speaking, Olaudah Equiano became

a spokesperson for the Black population in England. He was likely in contact with other notable speakers and writers of African descent, such as Charles Ignatius Sancho, Phyllis Wheatley and John Marrant. Equiano and Quobna Ottobah Cugoano formed the Sons of Africa, a Black abolitionist group, to advocate on behalf of their own people.

Following the Revolutionary War (1775–1783), which led to the founding of the United States of America, the population of Black people

Charles Ignatius Sancho was a free Black man known for his work as an abolitionist.

in Britain grew. As a wartime strategy, the British had offered freedom to any enslaved person who ran away from an American rebel enslaver and joined the Loyalist army. By the time the British lost the war, over twenty thousand people had freed themselves by escaping behind British lines. Some settled in Canada and the West Indies. Some decided to go on to England.

In England, life did not necessarily get easier. It was hard for free Black people to find jobs because they were competing with white British people in the same social and economic class, and only people who had been born in a British city could receive help from the local government. Some white British people across class groups saw the arrival of newly free Black people from the Americas as a problem. Others came up with a range of ideas to address the needs of the new Black British population. One of those plans involved resettling Black people in Africa.

115.

In August on my return
I was surprised to find
that the government planned
to send Africans to their native quarter,
to Sierra Leone,
an act which filled me
with prayers and rejoicing.

There was a select committee
of gentlemen for the black poor,
some of whom I had known.
As soon as they heard of my arrival
they sent for me.

They seemed to think me qualified
to superintend part of the undertaking,
to go with the black poor to Africa.
I pointed out to them many objections to my going
and particularly I expressed some difficulties
on the account of the slave dealers,
as I would certainly oppose their traffic
in the human species by every means in my power.

The gentlemen of the committee over-ruled,
and recommended me to act as commissary.
They appointed me in November 1786
to that office and gave me sufficient power
to act for the government.

Provisions for the voyage and after,
clothing, tools, and other articles
provided at the government's expense.

I proceeded immediately on board
vessels destined for the voyage,
as Commissary of Provisions and Stores
for the Black Poor going to Sierra Leone.

116.
During my employment
I was struck with the flagrant abuses
committed by the agent
and endeavoured to remedy them,
but without effect.
For instance, the government had ordered
all necessaries for 750 persons
however, not more than 426 to go,
I was ordered to send the superfluous
to the king's stores at Portsmouth.
When I demanded them from the agent,
it appeared they had not been bought,
though paid for by the government.

The people suffered infinitely more
their accommodations most wretched.
Many wanted beds, clothing, and other necessaries.

I could not silently suffer government to be thus cheated,
my countrymen plundered and oppressed,
left destitute.

I informed the Navy
of the agent's proceeding,
but was soon after dismissed from my duties.

They proceeded without me
and thus ended my part of the long-talked-of expedition
to Sierra Leone,
an expedition where there was evidently
sufficient mismanagement to defeat its success.

They reached Sierra Leone
at the season of the rains.
Impossible to cultivate the land,
their provisions were exhausted
before they could benefit from agriculture.
It is not surprising that many could not survive it.

The Sierra Leone Colony

ENGLAND HAD A GROWING POPULATION OF BLACK PEOPLE WHO
were unable to find work and facing poverty. Some abolitionists created a plan to set up a mixed-race colony of free Black people and some white people in Sierra Leone on the west coast of Africa, near where British business people still controlled Bunce Island. The British government and a group of abolitionists formed the Sierra Leone Company to manage the operation. One goal of the venture was to set up a more humane trade between Africa and England. The colonists would grow crops such as cotton and sugar to replace that produced by enslaved people across the Atlantic.

From the start, the program had issues. It was difficult to recruit the expected number of travelers. Mismanagement and corruption was also rampant, as Olaudah Equiano mentions in his book. The British government appointed him as the colony's commissary, the person in charge of supplies. This was the highest official role a Black British person had ever been assigned. When he discovered one of the company's agents had been stealing, he brought this to the attention of the leaders. A dispute followed, and Equiano eventually lost his position, though he claims in his memoir that people were satisfied with his work and he was still paid.

The group of settlers arrived in Sierra Leone and established their colony—called Granville Town after Granville Sharp—at the worst possible time. It was the rainy season, so they were unable to properly start farming. After a period of disease, hunger, hardship, and conflict with the local people who lived near the settlement, many settlers had died. The survivors eventually joined recruited people from Nova Scotia to settle a new colony called Freetown. Olaudah Equiano moved on to other activities that supported the abolitionist movement, such as speaking, debating and, of course, writing.

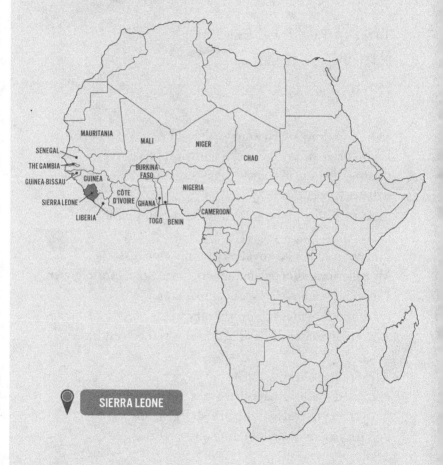

Sierra Leone is located on the west coast of Africa, bordered by Guinea to the north and Liberia in the south.

117.

On March the 21st, 1788,
I had the honour of presenting the Queen
with a petition on behalf of my African brethren,
which was received most graciously by her Majesty*:

To the QUEEN's most Excellent
Majesty.

MADAM,

YOUR Majesty's well known benevolence and humanity
Emboldens me to approach your royal presence,
trusting that the obscurity of my situation
will not prevent your Majesty
from attending to the sufferings for which I plead.

I do not solicit your royal pity for my own distress.
My sufferings, although numerous, are in a measure forgotten.
I supplicate your Majesty's compassion
for millions of my African countrymen,
who groan under the lash of tyranny in the West Indies.

The oppression and cruelty
exercised to the unhappy negroes there,
have at length reached the British legislature,
and they are now deliberating on its redress.

Your Majesty's reign has been hitherto
distinguished by private acts of benevolence and bounty;
surely the more extended the misery is,

the greater claim it has to your Majesty's compassion,
and the greater must be your Majesty's pleasure
in administering to its relief.

I presume, therefore, gracious Queen,
to implore your interposition with your royal consort,
in favour of the wretched Africans
that, by your Majesty's benevolent influence,
a period may now be put to their misery
and that they may be raised from the condition of brutes
to the rights and situation of freemen,
and admitted to partake of the blessings
of your Majesty's happy government.

So shall your Majesty enjoy the heart-felt pleasure
of procuring happiness to millions,
and be rewarded in the grateful prayers of themselves,
and of their posterity.

May the all-bountiful Creator shower on your Majesty,
and the Royal Family,
every blessing that this world can afford,
and every fulness of joy
which divine revelation has promised us in the next.

I am your Majesty's most dutiful and devoted servant to command,
GUSTAVUS VASSA,
The Oppressed Ethiopian.

Olaudah Equiano the Abolitionist

AFTER HE GAINED HIS OWN FREEDOM, OLAUDAH EQUIANO OCCASIONALLY tried to help other free Black people, but he also remained tied to the slave trade. He worked as a sailor on slave ships and helped buy, sell, and transport enslaved people. He also served as an overseer on a plantation. Gradually, he apparently realized that as long as the slave trade and slavery existed, his own freedom

Although he purchased his freedom in 1766, Equiano grew to realize that his own status was tied to the liberation of Black people globally. His book was one way he worked for the abolition of the slave trade.

was always in danger. He tells several stories about almost being kidnapped and resold before narrowly escaping. He recounts the stories of other free Black people he knew who were enslaved or re-enslaved. He began to speak out and to associate with the growing abolition movement in England. He tailored his messages to support the ongoing efforts of well-known allies: the Quakers, lawyer Granville Sharp, and Thomas Clarkson, who was writing, researching, and organizing for the growing coalition.

Olaudah Equiano timed the release of his book in 1789 to coincide with an important debate over slavery in Parliament. His eloquent voice as a survivor of slavery was unique at the time. It represented the lived experiences and aspirations of Black people, as well as their committed efforts to free themselves. Ultimately, the work of Olaudah Equiano and other abolitionists resulted in legislation that ended the slave trade. The emancipation of all enslaved people in British colonies around the world came several decades later.

118.

The renovation of liberty and justice rests
on the British government.
May the time come when the sable people
shall gratefully commemorate
the auspicious æra of extensive freedom.

I hope the slave trade will be abolished.

May Heaven make the senators the dispersers
of light, liberty, and science,
to the uttermost parts of the earth.

I hope the slave trade will be abolished.

Europe contains one hundred and twenty millions of inhabitants.
How many millions doth Africa contain?
If the blacks were permitted to remain
in their own country,
they would double themselves
every fifteen years.
The British manufacturer and merchant adventurer
will have a full and constant employ
supplying the African markets.

I hope the slave trade will be abolished.

Industry.
        Enterprise.
Mining.
        An endless field of commerce lays open.
        An inexhaustible source of wealth.

(Except those persons concerned
in the manufacturing of
neck-yokes,
collars,
chains,
hand-cuffs,
leg-bolts,
drags,
thumbscrews,
iron muzzles,
and coffins
and other instruments of torture
used in the slave trade).

The abolition of slavery would be a universal good.
I hope the slave trade will be abolished.

119.

I therefore request the reader's indulgence
and conclude.

I am far from the vanity of thinking
there is any merit in this narrative.

My life and fortune?
Chequered.
My adventures?
Various.

If any incident in this little work
should appear uninteresting,
almost every event of my life
made an impression on my mind
and influenced my conduct.

I look for the hand of God
in the minutest occurrence,
to learn from it a lesson of morality.
In this light every circumstance I have related
was of importance to me.

After all, what makes any event important,
unless by its observation we become
better and wiser?

Epilogue

AT THE TIME OF HIS BOOK'S PUBLICATION, EQUIANO WAS A well-known abolitionist who had become a spokesperson for British people of African descent. He wanted to convey the devastating horrors of slavery from his own perspective, in hopes that the British government would abolish both the slave trade and the entire system of slavery. Once the book was published, Equiano traveled around England and other nearby countries to promote it and to further spread the abolitionist message. His book sold many copies, and there were nine editions. It was printed as far away as the Netherlands, Germany, and the United States.

While on his book tour, he met Susannah Cullen, a white British woman from Cambridgeshire, and they married on April 7, 1792. Their interracial marriage was viewed as a respectable union for them both, and Equiano announced it in the fifth edition of his book. He was able to support his family as a writer and speaker. In fact, at the time of his death he was likely the wealthiest Briton of African descent. He was even able to leave an inheritance to his two daughters, Anna Maria and Joanna. He also designated money to fund missionaries and a school in Sierra Leone. He claimed to have earned this estate "by the sweat of my brow in some of the most remote and adverse corners of the world."

Olaudah Equiano died on March 31, 1797, as a freeman who had liberated himself against great odds. He had a complex relationship to the slave trade as both a former enslaved person and an active participant in the enslavement of others. He gradually embraced using the opportunities he had as an educated and well-connected person of African descent to advance the cause of abolition. Ultimately, he used his free status and his connections to work for the freedom of others.

England passed legislation to abolish the slave trade in 1807. The British Empire formally abolished slavery by passing an emancipation bill through Parliament in 1833. The British government agreed to pay enslavers for the loss of their workforce, which cost "the modern [2018] equivalent of about £17bn [$22 billion]." Those who had been enslaved received nothing. The United States did not abolish slavery until after the Civil War, when the US Congress passed the Thirteenth Amendment in 1865.

Olaudah Equiano's words were influential in documenting the horrors of slavery and ending it around the world. Today his words help us remember that history, tie it to the present, and continue working toward greater equality and justice.

Creating a Verse Version

This book is a novel-length series of found-verse poems crafted from Olaudah Equiano's original autobiography, *The Interesting Narrative of the Life of Olaudah Equiano, or Gustavus Vassa, the African*, published in March 1789. We have used both the first and ninth editions for this work. We wanted to provide an entry point into this essential primary source on the slave trade, slavery, and abolition for young readers. We wanted a new generation to be inspired by the arc of Equiano's experience from free child to captive to enslaved sailor to free adventurer and, ultimately, to abolitionist. We wanted young readers to be as enthralled and intrigued by his adventures as we have been.

A found poem is created using the words, phrases, and quotes from a source text that are then rearranged into verse. For this book, we went through the text and looked for Equiano's most glittering gems of phrasing and description. We crafted the poems solely from his words, molding them around poetic devices and forms. We added line breaks and stanzas for rhythm and clarity. The chapters align with those in the original. Titles are from key lines in the text.

Here is an example. The **bolded text** is used in the poem about Equiano's capture and separation from his sister. The poem follows after his text.

Come into the yard of our next neighbour but one, to kidnap, there being many stout young people in it. Immediately on this I gave the alarm of the rogue, and he was surrounded by the stoutest of them, who entangled him with cords, so that he could not escape till some of the grown people came and secured him. But alas! ere long it was my fate to be thus attacked, and to be carried off, **when none of the grown people were nigh. One day,** when all our people were gone out to their works as usual, and only I and **my dear sister** were left to mind the house, **two men and a woman got over our walls, and** in a moment **seized** us both, and, without giving us **time to cry out, or make resistance, they stopped our mouths, and ran off with us into the** nearest **wood.** Here **they tied our hands, and** continued to **carry us as far as they could, till night came** on, when we reached a small house, where the robbers halted for refreshment, and spent the night. We were then unbound, but were unable to take any food; and, being quite **overpowered by fatigue and grief, our only relief** was some **sleep,** which allayed our misfortune for a short time. The next morning **we** left the house, **and continued travelling** all the day. For a long time we had kept the woods, but at last we **came into a road** which **I believed I knew.** I had now some hopes of being delivered; for we had advanced but a little way before I discovered some **people at a distance,** on which I began to cry out **for** their **assistance:** but **my cries had** no other effect than to make **them tie me faster** and **stop my mouth**, and then they **put me into a large sack**. They also stopped my sister's mouth, and tied her hands; and in this manner we proceeded till we were out of the sight of these people. When we went to rest the following night they offered us some victuals; but we refused it; and the **only comfort** we had was in being in **one another's arms** all that night, and **bathing each other with our tears**. But alas! we were soon deprived of even the small comfort of weeping together. **The next day** proved a day of **greater sorrow than I had yet experienced**; for **my sister and I were then separated,** while we lay clasped in each other's arms. It was **in vain** that **we be**sought them not to part us; she was torn from me, and immediately **carried away**, while **I was left in a state** of distraction **not to be described.**

One day when none of the grown people were nigh
two men and a woman got over our walls,
seized my dear sister and me.
No time to cry out or make resistance.

They stopped our mouths,
and ran off with us into the woods.
They tied our hands and carried us
as far as they could, till night came.

Overpowered by fatigue and grief,
our only relief: sleep
our only comfort: one another's arms
bathing each other with our tears.

We continued travelling and came to a road
I believed I knew with people at a distance.
My cries for assistance had them
stop my mouth, tie me faster, put me into a large sack.

The next day: greater sorrow
than I had yet experienced.
My sister and I were separated.
In vain we sought them not to part us.

She was torn from me and carried away.
I was left in a state not to be described.

Timeline

1745 Olaudah Equiano is born in Essaka, in the kingdom of Benin (now southern Nigeria).

1756 Equiano and his sister are kidnapped by members of an invading tribe. They are subsequently separated and sold to various slave traders.

1757 Equiano is sold to a slave trader who forces him on a slave trading ship. This ship sends him to the island of Barbados, and later to a colony in Virginia. He is then shipped to England.

1758 Equiano becomes a servant of the British Navy during the Seven Years' War. He develops his skills as a sailor during this time.

1759 Equiano converts to Christianity. During his time as a servant on navy ships, he continues to experience various prominent battles as part of the Seven Years' War

1761 Equiano is present at the Capture of Belle Île on June 8.

1762 Lieutenant Michael Henry Pascal sells Equiano to Captain James Doran, who then sends him to Montserrat.

1763 Equiano arrives at Montserrat, where he is later sold to merchant Robert King.

1765 King sets Equiano's cost of emancipation at forty pounds.

1766 Equiano purchases his freedom on July 11 and continues to work on ships as a freeman.

1768 Equiano meets Dr. Charles Irving in England.

1773 Equiano travels to the North Pole with Irving and helps him develop a device to purify seawater.

1774 Equiano meets Granville Sharp.

1775 Irving recruits Equiano to travel to the Mosquito Coast in Central America.

1776 Equiano leaves the Mosquito Coast.

1777 Equiano moves to Plymouth, England.

1786 Equiano is appointed to the position of Commissary of Provisions and Stores for the Black Poor going to Sierra Leone.

1787 On May 22, the Society for Effecting the Abolition of the Slave Trade, a British abolitionist group, is founded.

1788 Britain passes the Slave Trade Act, which limits the number of enslaved people who could be carried on any given ship. It also set standards of treatment for enslaved people on ships.

1789 Equiano publishes his autobiography in March.

1792 On April 7, Equiano marries Susannah Cullen, an Englishwoman.

1793 Equiano's daughter Anna Maria is born on October 16.

1795 Equiano's second daughter, Joanna, is born on April 11.

1797 Equiano dies in London on March 31.

1807 Ten years after Equiano's death on March 25, the slave trade is abolished within the British Empire.

1834 The Slavery Abolition Act of 1833 goes into effect on August 4, outlawing all slavery in Britain and its colonies.

1865 The United States abolishes slavery with the ratification of the Thirteenth Amendment on December 6.

Glossary

apprentice: a person who learns a trade from a skilled employer, often for low or no wages

battery: a fortified area for guns and artillery

besought: begged for

broadside: when all the guns on one side of a ship are fired

burthen: burden

catgut: a cord made from animal intestines that can be used for instruments

chattel slavery: enslaving and owning a human being and their children as property

chilblain: inflammation of hands and feet due to exposure

citadel: a fortress

commodity: a product to trade

countenance: an expression of the face

cuff: to hit

cutwater: the front edge of a ship

edifice: a building

flogging: a beating with a whip or stick

gauging: to measure the dimensions of an object

grampus: a whale

guarda costa: coast guard

habeas corpus: the legal right to be brought before a judge or court

homage: respect

impressment: to seize someone into service, often military; also, press, press gang

indentured servant: a person obligated to work for someone for a specified amount of time

interest: money paid at a particular rate for the use of money lent

liberate: to free

man-of-war: a powerful warship

manumission: release from slavery

mariner: a sailor

mulatto: used to describe a person of mixed white and Black ancestry. This term is considered offensive, but it was not considered offensive in Equiano's time.

overseer: a person who supervises others, especially workers or enslaved people

philanthropist: a person who generously helps others, particularly with money

principal: main, also the original amount of a loan

prize: a captured enemy ship and its valuables

quadrant: a device used to determine the latitude at sea by measuring the height of a star or the sun

rhetoric: the art of speaking and writing effectively and persuasively

sea horse: an old English word for walrus

sloop: a one-masted sailboat

smallpox: a contagious and disfiguring disease that is now extinct due to immunization

tipstaff: a sheriff's officer or bailiff

venture: a risky investment; a daring journey

West Indies: the islands lying between southeastern North America and northern South America, bordering the Caribbean Sea and the Atlantic

Source Notes

18   Regarding the craftsmanship of the people of Benin: National Geographic Society, s.v. "The Kingdom of Benin," last updated May 20, 2020, https://education .nationalgeographic.org/resource/kingdom-benin/.

18   "Great Benin, where . . . to their houses.": Mawuna Koutonin, "Story of Cities #5: Benin City, the Mighty Medieval Capital Now Lost without Trace," *Guardian* (US edition), March 18, 2016, https://www.theguardian.com /cities/2016/mar/18/story-of-cities-5-benin-city-edo -nigeria-mighty-medieval-capital-lost-without-trace.

18   Trade between African people and Americas: National Geographic Society.

18   Equiano's birthplace: Vincent Carretta, *Equiano, The African: Biography of a Self-Made Man* (New York: Penguin, 2006), 2.

19   "civilized": Carretta, 5.

25   Slavery in 1000 BCE: Hugh Thomas, *The Slave Trade: The Story of the Atlantic Slave Trade; 1440–1870* (New York: Simon & Schuster, 1999), 44–46.

25   European socioeconomic classes: Carretta, 21.

25   Chattel slavery: Carretta, 22–23.

26   European enslavers waiting in coastal towns: Carretta, 19.

26   African leaders resisting slave trade: Thomas, 108.

26   Centuries of transatlantic slave trade and landscape of Africa: Thomas, 561–566.

32–33   Enslaving Indigenous Americans: Carretta, 22.

33   Laws against enslaving Indigenous peoples: Thomas, 286.

33   Twelve million Africans: Carretta, 18.

33   Global economy: Thomas, 286.

35   Bunce Island: David Olusoga, *Black and British: A Forgotten History* (London: Pan Macmillan, 2018), 1–6.

41   Twelve million Africans: Carretta, 18.

41   British ships: Olusoga, 202.

41   "Now the whole . . . almost inconceivable.": Olaudah Equiano, *The Interesting Narrative of the Life of Olaudah Equiano, or Gustavus Vassa, the African* (London: G. Vassa, 1789), 79.

42   Brookes: Adam Hochschild, *Bury the Chains: Prophets and Rebels in the Fight to Free an Empire's Slaves* (Boston: Houghton Mifflin, 2006), 155–156.

42   Zong court case: Hochschild, 79–81.

42   20 percent of British sailors died: Hochschild, 94.

42   1788 Slave Trade Act: Hochschild, 140.

45   Caribbean colonies: Hochschild, 55.

45   British colonies in the Caribbean: "Sugar Plantations," National Museums Liverpool, accessed August 19, 2021, https://www.liverpoolmuseums.org.uk/archaeologyofslavery/sugar-plantations.

45   England imports: Thomas, 481.

46   Replacing enslaved people: Hochschild, 67.

48   Barbados as key outpost: Hochschild, 61.

48   Trauma of unknown: Equiano, 61.

56   "the first successful . . . English-speaking world.": Carretta, 366.

60   England after Seven Years' War: History.com editors, "Seven Years' War," *History*, A&E Television Networks, last updated May 21, 2020, https://www.history.com/topics/france/seven-years-war.

60   Equiano at Battle of Quiberon Bay and the Siege of Louisbourg: Stephen Taylor, *Sons of the Waves: The Common Seaman in the Heroic Age of Sail, 1740–1840* (New Haven, CT: Yale University, 2021), 51.

60 Racial prejudice at sea: Taylor, 63.

66 Impressment, "press gangs": Taylor, xix.

66 One-third of all sailors: Hochschild, 222.

66 European society sympathetic: Hochschild, 225.

66 End of impressment: Taylor, 418.

90 Sugar production in Jamaica: Thomas, 275, 481.

91 Dangers of sugar production: "Sugar Plantations."

91 Sugar as England's largest import: Hochschild, 194.

91 Sugar boycott: Hochschild, 192–193, 195.

97 Toussaint L'Ouverture: Hochschild, 256–279.

97 Agreement with L'Ouverture: Hochschild, 279.

97 Uprisings: Olusoga, 203.

106 British economy benefits from slavery as a reason against emancipation: Carretta, 2.

106 Shipping companies and plantation owners: Thomas, 512–516.

106 Royal African Company: Olusoga, 73.

106 English worker concerns: Olivette Otele, *African Europeans: An Untold History* (New York: Basic Books, 2021), 78.

106 Death rate of white sailors: Hochschild, 94.

106 Groups recognizing the immorality of slavery: Thomas, 482.

106 Ending slave trade: Thomas, 493.

115 "Montserrat.—To all . . . TERRYLEGAY, Register.": Equiano, 99–100.

137 Apprenticeships: Tim Hitchcock et al., London Lives, 1690–1800, version 2.0, March 2018, https://www .londonlives.org/.

137 Jobs available to Black British people in the eighteenth century: Olusoga, 95–97.

150 Horatio Nelson: Kartikay Chadha et al., "Associates of Vassa." Equiano's World, last updated May 19, 2021, https://www.equianosworld.org/associates-family.php.

155 Court action: Thomas, 476.

159 Christians enslaving other Christians: Carretta, 80.

159   Dissenters: Carretta, 163.

159   Support of abolition from dissenter churches: Carretta, 168.

159   Countess of Huntingdon's Connexion: "Questioning Equiano." Equiano's World, accessed August 27, 2021, https://www.equianosworld.org/questioning.php.

160   Christian defense of enslaving humans: Carretta, 170.

164   Irving's ship captured by Spanish coast guard: Carretta, 180–181.

164   Equiano's participation in slavery in Igbo: Carretta, 184–185.

179   Free Black people in England: Carretta, 214–217.

179   Associates of Equiano: "Associates of Vassa." Equiano's World, accessed August 27, 2021, https://www .equianosworld.org/associates-family.php.

180   After the Revolutionary War: Olusoga, 158.

180   Resettling Black people in Africa: Carretta, 216–222.

184   Sierra Leone colony: Olusoga, 187.

184   Equiano as commissary: Olusoga, 176.

185   Freetown: Olusoga, 192–193.

186–187   "To the Queen . . . The Oppressed Ethiopian.": Equiano, 166–167.

189   Timing of Equiano's memoir: Carretta, 2.

194   Equiano as spokesperson: Carretta, 256.

194   "by the sweat . . . of the world.": Carretta, 364–367.

195   "the modern [2018] equivalent . . . [$22 billion].": David Olusoga, "The Treasury's Tweet Shows Slavery Is Still Misunderstood," *The Guardian,* February 12, 2018, https://www.theguardian.com/commentisfree/2018/feb /12/treasury-tweet-slavery-compensate-slave-owners.

197–198   "Come into the yard . . . to be described.": Equiano, 48–50.

Bibliography

"Associates of Vassa." Equiano's World. Last updated May 19, 2021. https://www.equianosworld.org/associates-family.php.

Carretta, Vincent. *Equiano, the African: Biography of a Self-Made Man*. New York: Penguin, 2006.

Costanzo, Angelo. *Surprizing Narrative: Olaudah Equiano and the Beginnings of Black Autobiography*. New York: Greenwood, 1987.

Equiano, Olaudah, and Vincent Carretta. *The Interesting Narrative and Other Writings*. Rev. ed. New York: Penguin Books, 2003.

History.com editors. "Seven Years' War." *History*, A&E Television Networks. Last updated May 21, 2020. https://www.history.com/topics/france/seven-years-war.

Hitchcock, Tim, Robert Shoemaker, Sharon Howard, and Jamie McLaughlin et al. London Lives, 1690–1800. Version 2.0, March 2018. https://www.londonlives.org/.

Hochschild, Adam. *Bury the Chains: Prophets and Rebels in the Fight to Free an Empire's Slaves*. Boston: Houghton Mifflin, 2006.

Koutonin, Mawuna. "Story of Cities #5: Benin City, the Mighty Medieval Capital Now Lost without Trace." *Guardian* (US edition), March 18, 2016. https://www.theguardian.com/cities/2016/mar/18/story-of-cities-5-benin-city-edo-nigeria-mighty-medieval-capital-lost-without-trace.

National Geographic Society. "The Kingdom of Benin." National Geographic Resource Library. Last updated June 9, 2020. https://education.nationalgeographic.org/resource/kingdom-benin/.

National Maritime Museum. "Bunce Island, Sierra Leone." Understanding Slavery Initiative. Accessed August 24, 2021. https://understandingslavery.com/artefact/bunce-island-sierra-leone/.

Olusoga, David. *Black and British: A Forgotten History*. London: Pan Macmillan, 2018.

Otele, Olivette. *African Europeans: An Untold History*. New York: Basic Books, 2021.

"Questioning Equiano." Equiano's World. Accessed August 27, 2021. https://www.equianosworld.org/questioning.php.

"Sugar Plantations." National Museum Liverpool. Accessed August 19, 2021. https://www.liverpoolmuseums.org.uk/archaeologyofslavery/sugar-plantations.

Taylor, Stephen. *Sons of the Waves: The Common Seaman in the Heroic Age of Sail, 1740–1840*. New Haven, CT: Yale University, 2021.

Thomas, Hugh. *The Slave Trade: The Story of the Atlantic Slave Trade, 1440–1870*. New York: Simon & Schuster, 1999.

Yale Macmillan Center. "Bunce Island History." The Gilder Lehrman Center for the Study of Slavery, Resistance, and Abolition, Yale University, 2004–2005 lecture. Accessed August 24, 2021. https://glc.yale.edu/lectures/evening-lectures/past-lectures/20042005/bunce-island/bunce-island-history.

Further Reading

Africa Is My Home by Monica Edinger (2013)

Africatown: America's Last Slave Ship and the Community It Created by Nick Tabor (2023)

African Town by Irene Latham and Charles Waters (2022)

The Classic Slave Narratives: The Life of Olaudah Equiano / The History of Mary Prince / Narrative of the Life of Frederick Douglass by Henry Louis Gates Jr., editor (1987)

Copper Sun by Sharon Draper (2006)

The Kidnapped Prince by Ann Cameron (2000)

Never Caught: The Story of Ona Judge (Young Readers Edition) by Erica Armstrong Dunbar and Kathleen Van Cleve (2020)

Olaudah Equiano: Journey on the Sea by Monica Reed (2021)

The Poet Slave of Cuba: A Biography of Juan Francisco Manzano by Margarita Engle (2011)

To Be a Slave by Julius Lester, illustrated by Tom Feelings (2000)

Index

Photo Acknowledgments

Image credits: IanDagnall Computing/Alamy Stock Photo, p. 6; Pictures From History/CPA Media Pte Ltd/Alamy Stock Photo, p. 19; KuroNekoNiyah/Wikimedia Commons (CC BY-SA 4.0) Gray Scale, p. 32; Library of Congress Prints and Photographs Division, p. 51; Print Collector/Hulton Archive/Getty Images, p. 90; Wikimedia Commons PD, pp. 96, 150, 155, 164; Digital Image Library/Alamy Stock Photo, p. 179; Gaulois_s/Shutterstock, p. 185; Album/British Library/Alamy Stock Photo, p. 188.

Design elements: backUp/Shutterstock.

Cover: incamerastock/Alamy Stock Photo; backUp/Shutterstock; Mockaroon/Unsplash.

About the Authors

MONICA EDINGER is an author and a retired classroom teacher. Her book *Africa Is My Home: A Child of the Amistad* won the 2014 Children's Africana Book Award. Monica is an influential voice in the children's book world with a large following on her blog, *educating alice*, at medinger.wordpress.com. She has contributed reviews and articles for the *Horn Book Magazine* and the *New York Times* and served on several award committees.

LESLEY YOUNGE is an author, mother, and middle school educator who is passionate about interdisciplinary education, experiential education, community engagement, and mindfulness. Lesley is also the author of *A-Train Allen* and shares her thoughts on writing, teaching, and curriculum at teacherlesley.com. She lives in Silver Spring, Maryland, with her family.